ARCHAEOLOGICAL THINKING

ARCHAEOLOGICAL THINKING

How to Make Sense of the Past

CHARLES E. ORSER, JR.

ROWMAN & LITTLEFIELD
Lanham • Boulder • New York • London

Published by Rowman & Littlefield
A wholly owned subsidiary of The Rowman & Littlefield Publishing Group, Inc.
4501 Forbes Boulevard, Suite 200, Lanham, Maryland 20706
www.rowman.com

Unit A, Whitacre Mews, 26-34 Stannary Street, London SE11 4AB, United Kingdom

British Library Cataloguing in Publication Information Available

Library of Congress Cataloging-in-Publication Data

Orser, Charles E.
  Archaeological thinking : how to make sense of the past / Charles E. Orser, Jr.
    pages cm
  Includes bibliographical references and index.
    ISBN 978-1-4422-2697-5 (cloth : alk. paper) — ISBN 978-1-4422-2698-2 (pbk. : alk. paper) — ISBN 978-1-4422-2699-9 (electronic) 1. Archaeology—Study and teaching. 2. Archaeology—Methodology. 3. Critical thinking—Study and teaching. I. Title.
  CC83.O77 2015
  930.1—dc23

                                                                    2014029696

∞™ The paper used in this publication meets the minimum requirements of American National Standard for Information Sciences—Permanence of Paper for Printed Library Materials, ANSI/NISO Z39.48-1992.

Printed in the United States of America

CONTENTS

Preface

THE IDEA FOR THIS BOOK DEVELOPED after years of teaching an undergraduate course on critical thinking in archaeology. The goal of the course was to examine how archaeologists create plausible interpretations of the past using scattered, fragmentary evidence. I always understood that most people interested in ancient history would never actually have the opportunity or desire to become professional archaeologists. Archaeology can be a difficult field, and fierce competition exists for the limited positions that are available. The scarcity of professional posts at museums and universities has always been smaller than the number of people available to fill them.

The examples I used in the course came mostly from the fringe side of archaeology. These outlandish, well-known examples of space aliens, sunken cities, and mysterious creatures were easy to analyze by comparing them with actual archaeological findings. My goal was never to debunk the examples per se but rather to help students learn to think critically about historically realistic alternatives.

That most of my students would never become professional archaeologists was not a deterrent. In fact, it impressed on me the importance of the course. Teaching the basics of archaeological thinking—what I call "archaeo-thinking"—would provide critical thinking skills students could use for the rest of their lives. Regardless of their eventual professions, all of them would confront outrageous interpretations of human history whenever they searched the Web, watched television, or read blogs. The development of the Internet and the expansion of cable television has been a boon to nonprofessional "archaeologists," individuals who have made a cottage industry of what they call "alternative history." As a result of their seemingly tireless efforts, a large number of people now think that humanity's accomplishments result from ancient interactions with space aliens, that Atlantis sunk in the middle of the Atlantic Ocean, and that early medieval monks once lived in North America.

After having taught the course for a few years, I realized that most people, even the well educated, can be susceptible to the yarns of nonprofessionally trained "archaeologists"—the pseudo-archaeologists. Individuals can be easily fooled if they have not developed the critical thinking skills needed to make their own, independent evaluations. The proponents of the most outlandish accounts are often well spoken, thoroughly convincing individuals who appear to present reasonable interpretations. That their views cannot be sustained with archaeological evidence does not deter them. Archaeologists know that ancient Britons built Stonehenge and that the Mayans constructed complex pyramids without any help from outer space. Human history is fascinating on its own terms, and no need exists to insert outrageous story lines into it.

I also discovered that a person does not necessarily need to have a great deal of archaeological knowledge to refute the most outlandish interpretations. Having such knowledge is certainly helpful, but all a person must do is engage in some archaeo-thinking: evaluate the claim, judge the assumptions, and consider alternative interpretations based on what archaeologists actually know.

As I mention in this book—and as every professional archaeologist knows—most of the silliest interpretations of the human story are harmless and easily refuted with archaeological evidence. But some of the most flawed, politically motivated interpretations can be extremely dangerous, and professional archaeologists have the duty to refute them quickly and completely.

Some professional archaeologists think it is beneath them to acknowledge the world of pseudo-archaeology, believing that it does not merit serious attention. Some of the ideas currently floating around on the Internet are so ridiculous that they do not deserve refutation. But the problem is that the general public may not feel the same way. A good story is always compelling, and the idea that our human ancestors once interbred with spacemen intrigues people throughout the world.

Education is the most effective means for combating the use of archaeology to create ridiculous or dangerous histories of humanity. But knowing precisely how archaeologists reach their conclusions—their thought processes and intellectual methods—is not widely known outside the profession. This book seeks to make some of the most basic thinking in archaeology available to a wide audience, including everyone who has never taken an archaeology course but who are nevertheless fascinated by our collective human story.

I attempt to present my arguments using straightforward language. I do not cover everything possible, and some professional archaeologists may find much of the content too simplistic for their liking. Simplicity and a lack of archaeological jargon was my goal. My view is that an explanation that cannot be understood is no explanation at all. Complex jargon may simply drive people to the more clearly spoken pseudo-archaeologists.

Numerous people have helped me as I prepared this book. I would like to acknowledge my first editor Wendi Schnaufer's initial belief in and enthusiasm for this book. Her encouragement was extremely gratifying. When Wendi left for another position, Andrea Offdenkamp Kendrick and Leanne Silverman assumed the editorship and maintained the same level of interest and encouragement. I thank them for seeing this book become a reality. Equally important are the original readers of the prospectus. Their insightful ideas considerably improved my presentation. Merilee Salmon, noted philosopher of science and well known to professional archaeologists, kindly read and commented on my logic chapter. Her guidance was crucial in helping me avoid a couple of serious mistakes. Archaeologist Ashley Smallwood of the University of West Georgia assisted me with understanding her important research. At the last minute, my daughter Christine saved my manuscript from the pernicious jaws of Word. Without her, I would still be retyping the manuscript. I sincerely appreciate everyone's kind help and guidance.

A large of number of individuals helped me obtain the images for this book. Many of them assisted me simply in the spirit of collegial kindness, and I deeply appreciate their help. They are Katherine Hull and Ron Williamson of ASI in Toronto; Marty Magne, Heidi Moses, and Suzanne Surgeson of Parks Canada; Jacqui Pearce of the Museum of London Archaeology; Julie Gribben of Osprey Publishing; Hannah Kendall of the Ashmolean Museum, Oxford; Günter Hägele of the University of Augsberg Library, Germany; Karin Zimmermann of the University of Heidelburg Library, Germany; Lorelei Corcoran of the University of Memphis; Don Hitchcock of Armidale, Australia; Mark Leone and Benjamin Skolnik of the University of Maryland College Park; and Nicholas Saunders of the University of Bristol, England.

I also wish to acknowledge my colleagues in the Department of Anthropology at Vanderbilt University. Everyone, especially Beth Conklin,

William Fowler, and Tom Dillehay, created a friendly environment for thinking, scholarship, and research. Their assistance has proven invaluable to me, and I deeply appreciate it. Last but certainly not least, I must acknowledge, as I always do, the encouragement, support, editorial abilities, and thoughtful ideas of Janice. Everyone who knows me understands the contribution she always makes to my research and writing, and, once again, her assistance has made this book considerably better than it would have been without her input.

What's This All About, Anyway?　　**1**
Thinking in Archaeology

I MAGINE THIS. YOU'VE HAD A LONG DAY at your job, in classes, or running errands, and you've decided to let things go for a while and just surf the Internet looking for interesting videos. You remember reading something in a blog mentioning the pyramids of Egypt, so you decide to find videos that might help you understand why the Egyptians built them. The first video you find is about Egypt's Great Pyramid of Giza (figure 1.1).

You decide to stick with this one for a while because the smooth-talking narrator, accompanied by a number of professional archaeologists, is explaining that the pyramid was built during the Fourth Dynasty as a tomb for Pharaoh Khufu. This means the pyramid is about 4,500 years old. A cut-away of the inside of the pyramid shows a series of shafts and chambers, two of which archaeologists have named the King's Chamber and the Queen's Chamber (figure 1.2). The archaeologists carefully explain what they know about Egyptian pyramids and explain that much still remains to be discovered by excavation. In fact, the narrator explains that archaeologists are hot on the trail of finding other tombs in the Valley of the Kings but that so far the Great Pyramid is the real gem. Its huge size proclaims how much the ancient Egyptians honored the pharaoh and tells us that they wanted his afterlife to be spent in grand style, surrounded by many beautiful things.

The Great Pyramid has fascinated the world for centuries. It has entered the human imagination and caused infinite wonder. Generations have marveled at how the pharaoh could have marshaled his power and authority to command his people to spend up to 12 years building this massive stone mountain in the middle of the Egyptian desert. The experts appearing in

Figure 1.1. The Great Pyramid at Giza, Egypt. © Darezare/Dreamstime.com.

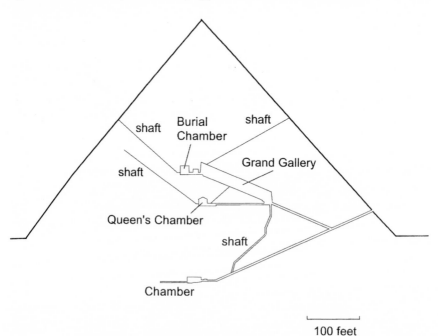

Figure 1.2. Inside the Great Pyramid showing the chambers and shafts. Adapted from John Romer, *The Great Pyramid: Ancient Egypt Revisited* (Cambridge: Cambridge University Press, 2007).

the video make it clear that the Great Pyramid is one of the world's most impressive historical monuments.

The video ends, and you've learned some interesting things about ancient Egypt and its Great Pyramid. But you notice that other videos have also been made about the Great Pyramid. Wondering what else there is to know about it, you click on another one. In this video, however, all that stuff about the pyramid being a burial vault for the pharaoh has disappeared. Now there's no mention of archaeological research or the results of any recent excavations. Instead, the narrator is saying that the pyramid was actually used to create nuclear energy! It wasn't a tomb at all; it was really a plutonium mill built by some mysterious, long-forgotten civilization. He says that archaeologists—like the ones in the first video—think Egyptians built it, but they're wrong. Ancient Egyptians had nothing to do with it. Just think about it, he says. Why would anyone build such a gigantic structure as a resting place for just one or two people, even if they were supposed to be semidivine? Why would so many people work so hard to build a pyramid when they could have built much smaller tombs or simply buried their dead under the sand? The sheer size of the pyramid implies a much more important function, doesn't it? As he says, the archaeologists' interpretation just doesn't make any sense.

Wow! This wasn't mentioned at all in the other show. The narrator of this video really seems to know what he's talking about. He's mentioning isotopes, Cesium-137, and Strontium-90, and he's convinced that building a huge pyramid for a few mummies is just silly. He also seems more enthusiastic than the professional archaeologists in the other video. Maybe he really has discovered a secret history, a story that no one knows.

So, having watched both videos, you're faced with an interesting situation. You've been given two competing interpretations about the purpose and meaning of the Great Pyramid. Both seem believable, and the presenters of each appear to have been knowledgeable. The nuclear guy seemed more scientific than the archaeologists because he mentioned the isotopes and such, but the archaeologists conduct excavations and historical research. The nuclear pyramid guy didn't mention anything about excavation or even Egyptian history for that matter. And then there was his enthusiasm and strong belief in his interpretation.

As the viewer, you are presented with ideas that are mutually exclusive: either ancient Egyptians built the pyramid as a tomb for their pharaoh, or some mysterious race built it as a nuclear plant. Both cannot be true, but how are you supposed to know which interpretation to accept? You cannot accept both because they are incompatible.

Puzzled but intrigued by the Great Pyramid, you begin to weigh the pros and cons of each video. In the first one, the professional archaeologists had spent years, sometimes their entire adult lives, trying to unravel the mysteries of the ancient Egyptians. You know that ancient Egyptian civilization is one of the most fascinating cultures that has ever existed, and you know from visiting museums that archaeologists have attributed some pretty incredible works of art to them. At the same time, though, you also know that archaeologists still don't know everything about ancient Egyptian life. You know because the archaeologists in the first video admitted it. True, they were extremely knowledgeable and dedicated, and they seemed to know what they were talking about. But, on the other hand, the nuclear fission guy was incredibly passionate and seemed to be equally honest and believable. In addition, he said all those scientific-sounding terms the archaeologists never even mentioned. He openly said that the archaeologists were wrong, but the archaeologists never mentioned the nuclear fission interpretation. Why not? Why didn't the archaeologists try to discount the man's atomic interpretation? Why did they just ignore it? Does this mean he's correct that professional archaeologists sometimes hide the truth about history? That they often cover up what they cannot explain?

What are you supposed to think? You're neither an archaeologist nor a nuclear scientist. You may become one or the other someday, but right now you're just interested in knowing the real story behind the Great Pyramid. You want to accept what the archaeologists said, but the science guy seemed so sure of himself. His conclusion suggested an undiscovered chapter of history, one that remains shrouded in the past. Could a mysterious, unknown civilization really have built nuclear facilities on earth even before the ancient Egyptian civilization had developed?

If you feel confused at this point, do not worry. All is not lost because it is possible to decide between the two interpretations using knowledge and reason. The good news is that you don't need to be a professional archaeologist to decide between the interpretations. You can make a reasonable decision based on a few simple skills.

This book is designed to give you the critical thinking skills to know how to decide between different interpretations. (I wanted to write "competing interpretations," but this would be inaccurate. For reasons that will become clear in this book, the interpretations do not really compete because only one of them—the archaeological one—is realistic. The other is nonsense.) With these skills, you will be able to think more clearly about the mysteries that still surround the human story. You will be able to think like an archaeologist—to practice archaeo-thinking—even though you might never find yourself in the bottom of an excavation trench in Egypt or on a mountaintop in Peru. As an intelligent consumer of science and history—on television, on National Public Radio, in newspapers, on blogs, on websites, and even on some future media yet to be invented—you will be constantly confronted with stories, articles, and videos about Egyptian and Mayan pyramids, ancient cities built with gigantic stones, archaeological sites revealing startling things, the statues on Easter Island, strange underwater structures, sunken civilizations, and hundreds of other subjects put forward by professional archaeologists, untrained men and women claiming to be archaeologists, and well-meaning scientists working outside their areas of expertise. As an archaeo-thinker, you will be able to disentangle the reasonable from the absurd and sort the plausible from the ridiculous. You will discover history as it was, not as we might wish it to have been.

A Question of Belief?

It is important to realize at the outset that this book is about critical thinking, not belief. The issue isn't what you believe because you are free to believe anything you wish. Belief does not require evidence, whereas archaeological interpretation relies on it. Without concrete evidence accepted by most members of the profession, archaeological interpretations are mere pseudo-archaeology. Pseudo-archaeology, sometimes termed "cult" or "fantastic" archaeology, is the presentation of often-outlandish views about human—and extraterrestrial (!)—history backed up with misunderstood or misrepresented evidence. The wildest interpretations are typically presented with no supporting evidence.

You may believe, for instance, that the world is flat, but it doesn't change the fact that Earth is not flat. Your flat-Earth belief doesn't change the evidence or affect your daily life unless you are a geologist or an astrophysicist. If you were an astrophysicist, the impact of your flat-Earth belief would be huge because your findings as a scientist would constantly contradict your belief. How could you calculate the time it would take for a satellite to orbit Earth if you thought the planet was flat? Even if you continued to hold firm in your belief, you must remain anchored, just like the rest of us, on the spinning oblate spheroid we call planet Earth. Your belief will neither affect gravity nor change its mysterious properties.

In *Thinking, Fast and Slow*, Nobel Prize–winning author Daniel Kahneman observes, "For some of our most important beliefs we have no evidence at all, except that people we love and trust hold these beliefs." So, if our fathers or mothers were flat-Earthers, we may choose to be one, too, despite the lack of evidence. But here we see the difference between belief and science: evidence for an interpretation must exist for science; they are not required for belief. Scientific discoveries cannot be accepted without acceptable proof, and scientific experiments are no good unless others can duplicate them and receive the same results.

The topic of this book, then, is about how archaeologists evaluate evidence and think in a way that allows them *to accept* (rather than *to believe*) accounts of history that make sense. All scholars, regardless of their fields of expertise or theoretical perspectives, are constantly faced with deciding among different interpretations. Knowledge expands and interpretations change as new evidence is collected and as concepts change. All scholars, including archaeologists, accept that their interpretations will be modified over time. Some of the once-most-cherished ideas may even be abandoned altogether. This is entirely normal.

Books written by today's archaeologists are one easy place to see the impact of the idea that interpretations change over time. In the not-too-distant past, archaeologists often began the title of their monographs with the word "The," as in *The Archaeology of [fill in the blank]*. Today, however, most archaeologists usually title their books *An Archaeology of [fill in the blank]*. Replacing the word "The" with "An" recognizes that the new account is the author's *interpretation* of a particular site's cultural history based on his or her perspectives, insights, interests, and careful evaluation of the available sources. A book called *The Archaeology of the Ancient Amazon* suggests that no more need ever be done on the subject, whereas a book titled *An Archaeology of the Ancient Amazon* implies that this book presents an interpretation based on the available evidence. Acknowledging that archaeological knowledge is accrued over time, the author does not claim to have written the final word on the subject. New knowledge will be obtained every time another archaeologist excavates in the Amazon Basin.

A new and thoroughly documented book of archaeological research, even one of exceptional quality, may not last forever as the ultimate interpretation. This is not to suggest that some interpretations do not stand the test of time. Some interpretations do remain the standard account for many years until enough information is gathered to permit its reassessment. Importantly, however, the switch from "The archaeology" to "An archaeology" is not meant to suggest that all interpretations have equal merit. Archaeologists know, because of the evidence they have recovered, that some interpretations are misinformed, misguided, or simply wrong. Professional archaeologists do not mention the atomic interpretation of the Great Pyramid because, without any evidence, it cannot compete with the long-accepted understanding that the pyramid was planned and constructed as the eternal resting place of an important pharaoh. It was not an atomic generator.

Proposing archaeological interpretations using different perspectives is perfectly normal because highly trained archaeologists disagree all the time. This does not mean, however, that anyone is being dishonest. Well-educated people can hold different views. New evidence can alter what archaeologists once thought they knew and change their ideas about people living in the past. As you will discover once you begin to archaeo-think, it is easy to decide between the most diverse interpretations, such as those of a professional Egyptologist and a nuclear scientist. It will be more difficult to decide between the interpretations of two professional archaeologists—who use substantiated evidence—but the process is the still same. This book teaches you how to make these decisions.

Science versus History

Is archaeology a science? You may have noticed that I began by mentioning scientists and then switched to writing about historians and archaeologists. I made the change on purpose because, as a discipline, archaeology stands midway between science and history. Today's archaeologists adopt methods, strategies, and ideas from both. Archaeology is not a hard science, like physics or chemistry, because archaeologists cannot re-create an ancient village and watch what the people living there do during the day. Archaeologists can only interpret the past based on their ideas coupled with the available evidence. As a result, archaeology is both a social science and one of the humanities.

If we think of science and the humanities as arranged on a continuum, we find some archaeologists describing themselves as being closer to the science end of the scale and others claiming to be closer to the history end. Most archaeologists would be somewhere in the middle, saying that they are both scientists and historians. Some archaeologists are very scientifically minded, and some are not. Some apply Darwinian selectionism to archaeological cultures and use highly sophisticated instruments in their research. Other archaeologists pore over faded documents and decipher hieroglyphs, seldom thinking about the complex statistics and high-tech equipment used by archaeological scientists. Regardless of their theoretical points of view, however, all professional archaeologists conduct excavations using systematic procedures rooted in scientific concepts of data collection.

The need for diligence, caution, and systematic methods is required during excavation because digging into the earth is a destructive process. When archaeologists conduct excavations, they disturb the soil layers, dig out storage pits, and remove artifacts. If archaeologists excavated ancient villages in a sloppy, unscientific manner, the evidence they acquired would be little better than that obtained by looters. As a result, archaeologists exercise extreme care when they excavate houses, villages, and settlements.

The science involved during excavation and the humanistic approaches often accessed during interpretation highlights the distinction between *detection* and *interpretation*. All archaeologists conducting fieldwork are equally engaged in detection. On approaching a village site or even an archaeological collection in a museum, every trained archaeologist should be able to detect the same things. Every individual should be able to recognize the potsherds, the arrowheads, and the pieces of metal in relatively the same way. Their skills in detection are honed through education and experience. Where they may differ, however, is in how they interpret the meaning of the artifacts. For example, does the transition from stone to brass arrowheads at a village site represent an acceptance of European culture, a technical understanding that metal is more efficient than stone, a change in spiritual beliefs, or some combination of several elements? Reasonable archaeologists, detecting the same artifacts, can present different interpretations.

Some of what we explore in this book will seem more dedicated to the science end of the scale than to the humanities end. This is because science teaches logic, reason, and evidence—all things that archaeologists need regardless of their expertise. Other subjects in the book relate more to historical analysis. The presentation of ideas from both science and the humanities demonstrates that today's archaeology is a multifaceted field with room for scholars having diverse interests, talents, and perspectives.

Thinking to Some Purpose

During the summer of 2007, while I was conducting excavations in Ireland, my wife and I were invited to the home of a BBC producer living in Northern Ireland. We had met her through a mutual friend, and we were excited to visit her for a number of reasons, one being that she and her husband, a well-respected attorney, were renovating a late eighteenth-century house. When we arrived and were shown around, we saw that the house was a historical treasure and that the couple were restoring it with loving care. During the evening, our host's husband, who had an interest in my research, mentioned a book he said had changed his life by making him a more effective attorney. This book was so important to him that he'd take it off the shelf every so often and reread parts of it. When he showed it to me, I was surprised to learn that it was not a dense legal tome but a small book of logic. It was only 191 pages, including the index, and it had been published as long ago as 1939! The title was *Thinking to Some*

Purpose, and its author was a long-deceased English philosopher named L. Susan Stebbing. (Wikipedia reports her first name as Lizzie, but I suppose that name doesn't suit a philosopher, so she just used the L!) My interest was piqued, and I filed the information away in my mind, hoping that someday I'd find a copy of this life-altering book. To my amazement, a couple of weeks later I actually did find a copy of the book in a used bookstore in Dublin.

According to Professor Stebbing (who died in 1943), the inspiration for the book came to her after delivering a lecture in 1936 to the annual conference of the British Institute of Adult Education. She titled her lecture "Thinking" because she believed that the mind of the average Briton was turning to mush. She said it was not enough for the British people to have a parliamentary government and freedom of the press; to enjoy the full benefits of democracy, they should also know how to think independently. As she states, "Our difficulties are due partly to our own stupidity, partly to the exploitation of that stupidity, and partly to our own prejudices and personal desires." Although blunt, Professor Stebbing's statement perfectly grasps three of the major obstacles to clear thinking:

1. Admitting what we don't know
2. Understanding how people take advantage of what we don't know
3. Acknowledging that we must not base our interpretations on what we may wish to be true or on our preconceived ideas

(In his book *Idiot America: How Stupidity Became a Virtue in the Land of the Free*, published in 2010—71 years after Stebbing's book first appeared— Charles Pierce makes the same case about the lack of thought among another citizenry. This time, however, the target is twenty-first-century Americans rather than early twentieth-century Britons!)

Stebbing begins by discussing politics and politicians, perhaps the one place where the three obstacles might be most easily observed. She quotes the words of the Lord Rector of the University of Edinburgh who in 1925 said that politicians and "advocates" (we'd say lawyers or possibly lobbyists) are more concerned with persuasion than proof. They are not necessarily dishonest, the Rector says; rather, they simply understand that the general public is unprepared to follow the average politician's arguments. As a result, the citizenry needs advocates to explain the arguments to them. Stebbing agrees with the Rector and adds her own evidence by quoting a speech mentioned in *The Times*. In 1937, a British statesman, extolling the virtues of the gloriously complicated British Constitution, is reported to have said that one of the reasons why the British people have enjoyed continued success and happiness was because they *"have never been guided by logic in anything."* (Professor Stebbing was so stunned by this observation that she put it in italics, as I have done here.) Properly aghast, she set out to remedy Britain's widespread lack of clear thinking in her little book.

Happily, ignorance is not a terminal condition. The professor says that we can all take action against it simply by training ourselves "to think effectively to some purpose." To do this, we must avoid two dangers. First, we must not rush into action without thinking. In other words, we must not accept something as a reasonable interpretation—that the Great Pyramid was a nuclear fission mill, for example—without carefully thinking it through. Second, and equally important, we must not develop an intellectual distance from life itself. Here she means that we should not bury ourselves in the history of ancient Egypt to the point of ignoring everything around us. Even competing interpretations—if based on evidence and logic—may have validity even if we disagree with them. Our task—as citizens and archaeologists—is to combine the ability to think clearly with a healthy dose of skepticism. Everyone can learn to do this because, as Professor Stebbing says, we all have "some capacity to follow an argument." We can all learn to think clearly.

The Process of Clear Thinking

The process of learning to think clearly begins with being puzzled about something. If we consider an explanation or interpretation to be implausible, if "it just doesn't sound right" to us, we must begin by thinking. We should not simply accept it without question. This is where skepticism is important. Once we are in a questioning frame of mind, we must seek answers to our questions. It helps to know a little something about the subject under consideration, but prior knowledge is not always essential. For instance, you probably already suspect that ancient Egypt was not the site of a nuclear energy plant. You may want to believe in this mysterious history, but you probably suspect, if you just think about it, that the atomic interpretation is pure fantasy. Still, you may not be entirely certain. You would be on firmer ground if you knew that ancient Egypt was home to a well-organized, sophisticated civilization (i.e., did not need alien intervention), but you don't necessarily need this information to judge the nuclear interpretation unrealistic. You simply need to wonder why the nuclear interpretation man did not present any physical evidence or artifacts to support his view. If you remember seeing Egyptian artifacts in museums, you could use this supporting knowledge to ask why the museum did not exhibit any atomic artifacts. The more you know, the more sure you can be in your assessment. Skepticism will help you ask questions and wonder about evidence even if you do not have abundant amounts of prior knowledge at your fingertips.

Stebbing observes that no thinking person can knowingly accept two competing interpretations at the same time. We cannot decide that the Great Pyramid was both a tomb and a plutonium generator. The way forward is to recognize that the interpretations are contradictory and then puzzle our way through each. To do this, we can pose a series of questions to help us resolve our confusion. The answers we receive will allow us to reject one of the interpretations.

Stebbing relates the story of a little boy playing on the floor with an electric train. The boy puts the train on the metal tracks expecting it to move, but nothing happens. Working out a solution, he picks up the engine, goes to the cupboard, takes down a can of oil, and lubricates the wheels. He sets the engine back on the tracks, but still nothing happens. Although he has achieved no results, the little boy's actions demonstrate intelligence because he has used knowledge to oil the train's wheels when it refuses to move. Oiling has worked in the past. This time, though, his approach was unsatisfactory because oil was not the problem; the train's battery had simply run down. The boy didn't know about batteries or how they worked, so his lack of experience and knowledge failed him. His failure does not mean that he is unintelligent, only that he made the wrong interpretation because he didn't have all the necessary information. In any case, his willingness to seek a reasonable solution is admirable even though he failed to make the train move.

The same is true in the case of the Great Pyramid. How can professional archaeologists so easily reject the claim of the nuclear scientist to the point that they do not even mention it in their videos, books, and lectures? And, conversely, why does the nuclear scientist feel he must mention that his interpretation differs from that of the entire archaeological profession? Is he simply trying to show that he's a bold, original thinker, or does he really believe he's discovered the truth by being unconventional? The answers to these questions lie in the ability to engage in archaeo-thinking. That an outlandish nuclear interpretation about the Great Pyramid, one of the Seven Wonders of the Ancient World, can be believed by millions of otherwise thinking people tells us that we need the guidance of people like Professor Stebbing.

A short introduction to the history of thinking in archaeology will help orient you to the subject and show that interpretations change over time as individual researchers think and learn more. This background information will help show you the importance of thinking like an archaeologist.

A Brief History of Archaeo-Thinking

The Early Years

The practice of archaeology began during the Renaissance, when wealthy men and women discovered an interest in ancient things and storied places. As the elites of European society—and trained in the classics—they had the leisure time to walk among the ruins at Pompeii, to sail among the Greek islands, and to visit the standing stones on Salisbury Plain. Not being trained as archaeologists—because the profession did not exist at the time—these amateurs' interpretations were usually composed of a mixture of intuition, wishful thinking, and fantasy. The earliest archaeologists seldom dug into the earth, but when they did, their excavations were usually reckless and not well planned. Even the most well meaning and careful among them could not consult scientific archaeological journals and reports because such resources simply did not exist. As a result, the earliest archaeo-thinking was generally characterized by two general themes: a romance for the past and an aesthetic love of beautiful objects.

In the late eighteenth and early nineteenth centuries, wealthy, educated Europeans romanticized Greek and Roman history and demonstrated their fascination with these civilizations in their architectural designs, fraternal organizations, and literature. For example, writer Edward Bulwer-Lytton played on the romance of the classical past by drawing on Pompeii, one of the most fabled cities of the ancient world. Spectacularly destroyed by an earthquake in 79 CE, this ash-smothered city was the quintessential archaeological site of the day, and it fascinated just about everyone who learned of it. Bulwer-Lytton's completely fictitious book *The Last Days of Pompeii*, published in 1834, presents a romantic view of life in the city as he imagined it. On visiting Pompeii, he had become enthralled by what he called "those disinterred remains," and his goal was "to people once more those deserted streets, to repair those graceful ruins, to reanimate the bones which were yet spared to his survey; to traverse the gulf of eighteen centuries, and to wake a second existence—the City of the Dead!" Bulwer-Lytton was happy to supply European readers with romantic, imaginary tales that had no connection to the actual history of the city.

Beautiful objects, such as the red and black terra-cotta Greek vases to be found on display in the British Museum and all the other great museums of Europe, equally fascinated the public with their beautifully intricate designs. The public was so taken with the artistic marvels of the ancient world that Josiah Wedgwood, the famous English potter (see chapter 7), made his first fortune by selling finely made bowls, vases, and jars embossed with Greek and Egyptian designs.

The United States, of course, had no classical Greek or Roman history, so the nation's antiquarians sought to investigate the ancient past at home. Since their earliest days on the continent, European settlers had been amazed by the earthen mounds dotting the countryside. The great heaps of earth—some rounded, others flat topped—were North America's pyramids. No one living at the time—incoming European or indigenous Native American—knew who had built them, how, or even why. The nation's early archaeologists simply called their makers "The Mound Builders," and many people became obsessed with solving the mystery of their identity.

Biased ideas about American Indians led many of the country's earliest antiquarians to conclude that the continent's native peoples were simply incapable of building such magnificent structures. Having discounted America's oldest inhabitants as the mounds' architects, scholars sought to identify other builders. Some named the Lost Tribes of Israel, but others settled on the Romans, the Vikings, the Phoenicians, and a host of others. The most creative argued that the mounds were the products of an undiscovered civilization, one completely unknown to recorded history. For them, the term "Mound Builder" was perfect because it represented an entirely new culture, yet undiscovered and unnamed.

America's earliest archaeological scholars were thinking, but they were not archaeo-thinking. They were allowing their biases and preconceptions to guide their research. As Stebbing observes, some people confuse logical thinking with "attempting to derive knowledge about what happens in the world by purely *a priori* [beforehand] speculation. Such an attempt is, however, thoroughly illogical; it is anti-scientific." The earliest thinkers about America's Mound Builders based their interpretations on speculation rather than evidence.

The trend in the United States away from loose speculation and toward archaeological evidence began to change because of Thomas Jefferson's high-profile research in Virginia. Jefferson was the most famous American to express an opinion about the true identity of the Mound Builders. Like many eighteenth-century scholar/scientists, Jefferson had read about the controversy, but unlike many of his contemporaries—men who were happy espousing their ideas from the comfort of their parlors—he sought to find answers through excavation. Writing in his *Notes on the State of Virginia*, Jefferson recounted his investigation of an Indian mound—which in European fashion he termed a "barrow"—on the Rivanna River in central Virginia. Jefferson's measured account obscures the excitement he must have felt when he discovered bones inside the mound. This irrefutable evidence led him to conclude that ancient Native Americas had constructed the mounds. Even he, however, left some room for doubt. In a curious footnote, he wrote, "The custom of burying the dead in barrows was anciently very prevalent. Homer describes the ceremony of raising one by the Greeks. . . . And Herodotus . . . mentions an instance of the same practice in the army of Xerxes on the death of Artachæas [Achaemenes]." Comments such as these, from one of the nation's most revered amateur scientists, demonstrate how poorly formed was the day's archaeo-thinking. Jefferson used his empirical findings to frame his interpretations, yet he still clung to poor archaeo-thinking by making reference to ancient Greek history when writing about ancient North America.

Comments by such a learned gentleman as Jefferson fueled the imaginations of many others who wanted to believe in a mysterious past, one that linked the ancient histories of the Old and New Worlds. The universal similarity among all earthen mounds and ancient pyramids kept alive the concept of a mysterious Mound Builder "race." Some speculators were led to ask, If both the ancient Greeks and the ancient Americans had built earthen mounds, could they be the same people or at least have the same ancient ancestor?

Stories of an advanced, unknown "race" continued to circulate through the taverns, general stores, and parlors of the embryonic United States. Only a couple of years before Jefferson wrote his *Notes*, James Adair, an Indian trader originally from the north of Ireland, published a history of the American Indians. Taking note of the Mound Builder controversy, Adair observed that most of his contemporaries believed that America's Indians derived from one of three peoples: "Pre-Adamites," "a separate race of men," or the Chinese. Unlike many others who would follow him, Adair was not convinced that any of these people, even the "separate race of men," were actually responsible for the mounds. Instead, he believed that America's native peoples were descended from the Jews, and he gave 23 reasons to support his conclusion. In 176 pages, Adair compared selected cultural elements—including the idea of tribal organization, the mode of religious observation, and the use of bodily ornamentation—to reinforce his view of a Native American–Jewish connection. His interpretation, however, rested on pure speculation; he had no concrete information to support his view.

The debate about America's mounds was still alive at the start of the nineteenth century. The failure of antiquarians to devise an agreed-on interpretation led Caleb Atwater to compile the first systematic account of the mounds in the eastern United States. A postmaster by profession and an amateur archaeologist by choice, Atwater did not believe that Native Americans had built the mounds. His choice was the Tatars from southern Asia or possibly even "Hindoos." He conceded that Native Americans had left tangible remains on the landscape—artifacts and settlements—but said that they were "neither numerous nor very interesting." Atwater figured that one way to solve the problem of the Mound Builders was to discover where they had gone. If the mounds' architects were not American Indians, then what had happened to them? They must have gone somewhere, leaving the continent to the various Indian cultures. He decided that the Mound Builders must have gone to South America, one place where other mounds (both stone pyramids and earthen mounds) could be found.

Despite Atwater's misguided ideas about the mounds' histories, he made a lasting contribution to North American archaeology by drawing a scale map of the earthworks at Circleville, Ohio. This earthwork was especially intriguing because it had been built in a perfect circle with a equilateral square attached to its eastern side. Atwater's scale drawing became a model for the most famous early nineteenth-century study of the earthen structures in the eastern United States: *Ancient Monuments of the Mississippi Valley* by Ephraim G. Squier and Edwin H. Davis, published in 1848.

The publication of Squier and Davis's *Ancient Monuments* was the seminal event of early nineteenth-century archaeology. It paved the way for the full-blown development of American archaeology and made modern archaeo-thinking possible despite the authors' misguided interpretations. Like many of their contemporaries, neither Squier (a journalist) nor Davis (a physician) had any archaeological training. Their faculties of detection were impeccable, but their interpretations were based on the speculation typical of the era.

The Middle Years

Squier and Davis's service to archaeo-thinking was twofold. First, they promoted the systematic, careful investigation of archaeological sites, and, second, they executed a number of bird's-eye-view, scale drawings of several mounds in the central United States (figure 1.3).

These drawings are so good that archaeologists still refer to them today. Unfortunately, their contribution to modern archaeology was purely methodological because their interpretations were merely speculative. Their field research did not lead them to the correct interpretation about America's mounds. Rather, they decided that the "Mound Builders" were neither the ancestors of America's Indian peoples nor the Jews, Tatars, or Hindus; they were a separate people altogether. But in an early indication that archaeology would eventually abandon pure speculation for a reliance on evidence, Squier and Davis observed that the earthen mounds could be used to provide conclusive proof about the Mound Builders' history and culture. The design and composition of the mounds

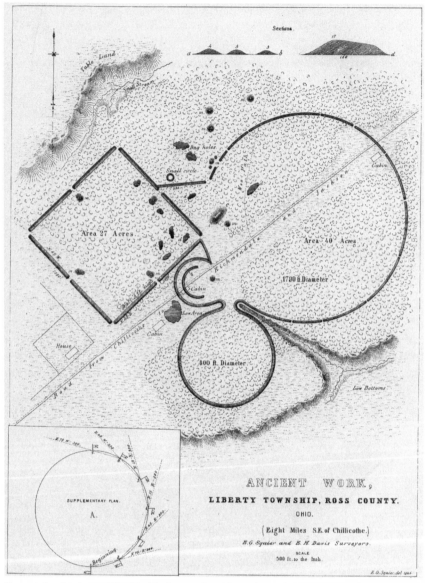

Figure 1.3.   Squier and Davis's 1846 map of "High Bank Works," Ross Co., Ohio. In *Ancient Monuments of the Mississippi Valley: Comprising the Results of Extensive Original Surveys and Explorations* by Ephraim G. Squier and Edwin H. Davis, Smithsonian Contributions to Knowledge, vol. 1 (Washington, DC: Smithsonian Institution, 1848), facing p. 50.

clearly indicated, they said, that the Mound Builders had developed advanced agriculture and complex decorative arts as well as organized customs and religious beliefs. They argued that without these cultural traits, the Mound Builders would not have been organized enough to build the most intricate mounds. For them, ancient Native Americans could not have been the mounds' architects because the Mound Builders had been industrious and settled, whereas Indians were "averse to labor." Squier and Davis's perception that Native Americans were lazy did not permit them to see ancient Indians as the builders of the mounds. The two men, however, did reach some of the right conclusions. They were correct that America's Mound Builders were agricultural peoples who had developed complex cultural traits, including intricate social hierarchies, religious concepts, and kinship systems.

Squier and Davis had reached some of the right conclusions, even though their biased views of nineteenth-century Native Americans influenced their interpretation. Squier and Davis's ill-devised speculations caused them to ignore the obvious. At the time, no one then had any physical evidence of the mysterious race they conjured up, and no one to this day has ever found any.

Archaeologists solved the Mound Builder controversy by about 1880, with the conclusion being the most obvious one: that the Mound Builders were the ancestors of today's Native American peoples. An early scholar who made this case was Cyrus Thomas, a professional archaeologist employed by the Bureau of Ethnology, a governmental agency dedicated to scientific, cultural, and historical research. In *Work in Mound Exploration of the Bureau of Ethnology*, published in 1887, Thomas moved professional archaeology away from mere speculation for all time. He called for archaeologists to study "the languages, customs, art, beliefs, and folk-lore of the aborigines" in addition to their ancient remains. He believed that only through comprehensive investigation could archaeologists demonstrate the obvious historical link between nineteenth-century Native Americans and the ancient remains found throughout the eastern part of the United States.

Thomas could not have been any more clear, but even today a few pseudo-archaeologists (untrained, nonexcavating speculators about human history) continue to espouse controversies like the Mound Builders. Such speculators continue the tradition of late eighteenth- and early nineteenth-century thinking. Their ideas are often outlandish and even ridiculous. Even so, they can often serve as good lessons because they represent the opposite of archaeo-thinking.

The Recent Years

By the beginning of the twentieth century, American archaeologists had begun to employ archaeo-thinking in ways that are familiar today. For most of the century, North American archaeologists used the artifacts they excavated and studied to construct large-scale cultural histories of native North America. These histories, when added to accounts compiled with written records, would present the entire story of the continent's indigenous cultures.

In order to write the regionwide histories, twentieth-century archaeologists first had to make certain that they had thoroughly and unambiguously described the artifacts from each period of history. Only through careful description could they communicate with one another about what they had found in their excavations. The thorough description of artifacts, compiled with scientific accuracy, was the first true step to good archaeological thinking. Using a comparative method, then, they were able to piece together the history of ancient North America without having to rely on supposition. They used actual physical things from the past to help them write ancient history.

SERIATION

The development of seriation in the early twentieth century represents one of the earliest expressions of good archaeo-thinking. Seriation allowed archaeologists to use the proportions and ages of artifacts to guide their chronological and cultural interpretations. The method's quantitative aspect proved that empty speculation had no place in professional archaeology.

During the 1910s, archaeologists excavating in the American Southwest experimented with ways of placing artifacts—mostly potsherds—into chronological sequences based on their physical characteristics. Two archaeologists in particular, N. C. Nelson and Leslie Spier, had independently found seriation to be useful in helping them work out regional cultural histories. Both of them sought to understand the sequence of pueblo history by placing potsherds in chronological order based on the sherds' observable characteristics. Using this method, each man discovered that existing pottery types disappeared over time as new styles appeared. By examining the percentages of each type, they were able to "seriate" (to arrange in a series) the various ancient potsherds chronologically.

Nelson and Spier each had difficulty deciding how to present the complex information they had compiled using seriation. Percentages of pottery types reported in tables and shown in line graphs failed to display the process of historical change. The numbers were too sterile to convey the significance of cultural change. By the 1940s, however, archaeologists had discovered how to present seriation visually.

The percentages of each pottery type, as they persist through time, approximate a battleship-shaped curve. This means that when the percentage of a type's distribution is represented vertically on a graph (with time on the vertical axis), both its starting and its end points are thin (when the pottery was first introduced and when it was dying out). The midpoint is thick (its percentage is high) because this is when the ware was most popular. Once an archaeologist has worked out the introduction, popularity, and demise of each pottery type (as indicated by the change in percentages over time), he or she can arrange them into a historical sequence.

A hypothetical example using Spier's pottery types shows how archaeologists illustrate the method (figure 1.4). In the example are six archaeological sites, dating somewhere between 1000 and 1400 CE, and five pottery types. The sites are arranged vertically from earliest to most recent, and the percentages of pottery types found at each site are represented by black blocks. The pottery for each site equals 100 percent (adding from left to right). In Site 1, black-on-white pottery accounts for 98 percent of the collection and corrugated pottery for 2 percent. In Site 2, the percentage of black-on-white pottery sherds has slightly decreased, and the corrugated ware has slightly increased. At Site 3, corrugated pottery was the most popular, and black-on-white pottery has shrunk to only 30 percent. By the date of Site 6, black-on-white pottery has been completely replaced. It disappears from the collection.

Using this concept and the potsherds from his 167 sites, Spier concluded that the earliest pueblo ruins were those with 96 to 98 percent black-on-white painted sherds and 2 to 4 percent corrugated wares. At later sites, the black-on-white sherds decreased to about 30 percent, and the percentage of corrugated pieces increased. At this time, a new type, redware, accounted for 43 percent of the pottery collection. Corrugated wares decreased from 50 to 55 percent to 30 percent, and another ware, whiteware, decreased from 45 to 50 percent to 20 percent. At this time another new ware, called buffware, appeared.

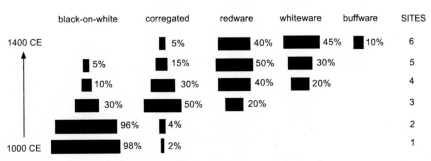

Figure 1.4.   Hypothetical seriation of five pottery types over time.

Seriation represents a good example of archaeo-thinking. Using this method, which can become extremely complicated for large numbers of sites occupied for long periods, archaeologists can use the physical remains along with their knowledge of culture and history to guide their conclusions. The resultant interpretations, though they may prove to be incorrect, nonetheless rely on careful collection, observation, analysis, and study. No place exists for mere speculation.

THE CONJUNCTIVE APPROACH

The development of seriation marked an important event in the history of archaeo-thinking, and in the 1940s another milestone occurred with the publication in 1948 of Walter Taylor's *A Study of Archaeology*. This book is significant because Taylor challenged archaeologists to modify how they thought about their field. He said that in their efforts to write detailed artifact descriptions and create large-scale chronologies—including by using complex seriations—archaeologists had gotten too far away from their anthropological roots. By being too single-minded about chronologies, archaeologists had stopped archaeo-thinking too early. They had created reliable histories of past Native American cultures, but they had overlooked the cultural dynamics of the people themselves. They had eliminated the active lives of the peoples by placing their emphasis on artifact descriptions and the construction of historical periods.

Taylor's answer to the problem, which he called the "conjunctive approach," was a six-step plan of research. His process began by identifying the questions to be addressed. This stage involved at least two basic queries each archaeologist should ask: what do they want to find out, and where is the best place to discover it? Once an archaeologist has answered these questions, the second stage involves collecting, describing, analyzing, and interpreting the amassed information. By "information," Taylor meant all pertinent factors that might have influenced a culture's history: the geology, the weather, cultural practices and traditions, historical trends, and so forth. This stage involved both fieldwork and laboratory-based analysis. In the third stage, the archaeologist should create the historical chronology from the evidence collected during the second stage, and in the fourth stage, he or she should synthesize the information. The fifth stage involves the comparative study of similar cultures to discover broad similarities and differences between them. Using what has been learned in the preceding stages to understand the "nature and workings" of culture in general constitutes the final state of Taylor's research process.

The conjunctive approach represented an important shift in archaeo-thinking because it presented, as Taylor noted, "a conceptual scheme made explicit in a set of goals." His central point was that archaeologists should seek to understand the dynamics of culture rather than to reduce culture to a series of historical sequences represented by a few key artifacts. For him, the creation of complex chronologies is only one step in a much larger anthropological project to understand culture. Rather than viewing history as a static collection of artifacts arranged in a neat order, Taylor encouraged archaeologists to perceive past cultures as alive and active. Seriation was a tool that archaeologists could use to understand ancient cultures, but it was not an end in itself. Taylor saw archaeology as a technique that anthropologically trained archaeologists could use to collect cultural information about the past. One notable aspect of his approach is that most of the process involved consciously thinking through a problem that archaeological research could be used to investigate. Professor Stebbing would have recognized that Taylor and the archaeologists who followed his advice were thinking to some purpose.

Taylor's views were controversial, but they continued to percolate within the archaeological community in the late 1950s as his anthropological perspective slowly gained ground. By the late 1960s, his views were presented again in what came to be called the New Archaeology (often spelled "archeology" to show that it really was something new). In the United States, the main proponent of the new approach was Lewis Binford.

In a famous article titled "Archaeology as Anthropology," Binford reiterated Taylor's thinking by observing that "until we as archaeologists begin thinking of our data in terms of total cultural systems, many . . . prehistoric 'enigmas' will remain unexplained." The time for Taylor's views had arrived, and the new thinking was so significant that many archaeologists dubbed it a "revolution" in the field.

The New Archaeology was also called "processual archaeology" because its designers sought to examine the processes of past daily life. Once archaeologists started thinking about past cultures as dynamic institutions, they confronted ponderous questions: How can archaeologists observe human activity in inert pieces of broken pottery, pieces of gunflints, and dusty old fire pits? How can they see cultural processes in action when all the people they study have long since died? How do archaeologist re-create life from inanimate artifacts and deteriorated building remains? These questions required serious contemplation and reflection because they reached into the very soul of archaeological research. They were so profound, in fact, that even philosophers of science began to ponder them.

The introduction of philosophers to archaeo-thinking meant that archaeologists began to explore topics entirely new to them. They started to think about creating hypotheses and to ponder how they could best test them, they began to explore various methods of observation and explana-tion, and they started wondering whether they could discover and identify general laws of human behavior. This period of philosophical reflection was a major advance in archaeo-thinking because it brought to the fore explicit ideas about logical argumentation and the need for the creation of systematic research designs.

The conscientious urge to make archaeology more overtly scientific and philosophical promoted the cause of thinking to some purpose. Twen-tieth-century archaeologists had left antiquarianism far behind as they truly became social scientists of history. The transition from history to science, however, was not without problem.

After a few years of attempting to apply what they had learned from both philosophers of science and physical scientists, some archaeologists began to think that the strict application of the scientific method had put their research into an intellectual straitjacket. Some began to wonder whether too many archaeologists had become philosophical theorizers rather than excavators. Skeptics thought that too many of their colleagues, by turning to the phi-losophy of archaeological science, had given the dynamics of culture and history short shrift. In moving closer to the science end of the continuum, they had gotten too far away from the historical end.

As a result, by the 1980s, many archaeologists had begun to reassert their interests in social, cultural, and historical dynamics, saying that they wanted to be archaeologists, not philosophers. What occurred, then, was a shift away from the rigid hypothesis testing of the late 1960s and 1970s but a retention of the scientific requirement of logic and rigor. This less rigidly scientific archaeology is generally known as "postprocessual" archaeology. Professional archaeology would never return to the days of speculation, but it was clear that many archaeologists sought a thoughtful combination of logical thinking and scientific methods (from processual archaeology) and cultural sensitivity and historical awareness (from the disciplines of cultural anthropology and social history).

Postprocessual archaeology, the archaeology of the twenty-first cen-tury, is thus perhaps best perceived as an anthropological/historical dis-cipline. Today's archaeologists retain their interests in social and cultural processes while adopting concepts and perspectives from a vast array of related disciplines, including women's studies, critical race theory, and postcolonial theory, among others.

Postmodern Thinking

One detour in archaeo-thinking appeared in the 1980s and 1990s as a num-ber of archaeologists were drawn to postmodernism, a school of thought with roots in the 1950s. Postmodernism is a complex collection of philosophical perspectives that propose that all knowledge is culturally conditioned and often politically motivated. Postmodernists argue that the methods and perspectives of the Enlightenment—the rational, scientific philosophy of the modern age—must be overcome with new ways of thinking. Postmodern thinking in archaeology has always been controversial.

Postmodern thinking has had some benefits to archaeology. For instance, by arguing that all perspectives have equal merit, postmodernism opened the minds of archaeologists and allowed them to consider the validity of indigenous peoples' traditions and oral accounts. Beforehand, many archaeologists may have too readily dismissed a people's oral history as irrelevant to archaeological analysis. Much of this intellectual rigidity is now gone from the discipline, as today's archaeologists are likely to engage in dialogues with native peoples rather than to scorn their accounts as unimportant. Such conversations have promoted cross-cultural understandings and have led to a number of collaborative projects between archaeologists and community members.

The postmodern thinking that accompanied some postprocessual archaeology also had at least two detrimental effects. First, many radical postmodernists argued that objective truth does not exist. Extreme postmodernists say that we only fool ourselves when we think we can know anything objectively, especially where the past is concerned. They argue that objective truth is a mirage, that all accounts perpetuate an agenda of some sort. They propose that archaeological knowledge is as valid as traditional knowledge.

These critics have a point; objectivity can be a knotty problem where native traditions are involved. Common ground may be difficult to establish when a people's traditions conflict with archaeological findings. The two interpretations may be incompatible when one is based on belief and the other is rooted in empirical evidence. American archaeologists, trained as anthropologists, accept that religious beliefs are distinct from archaeological findings, but as archaeologists thinking to some purpose, they must follow the empirical evidence while simultaneously being sensitive to the traditional beliefs.

One challenge facing today's archaeologists is to ensure that their findings are not used against native peoples. Many ancestral homelands might have considerable economic value, and any effort by archaeologists to argue that the lands are not sacred can be condemned as cultural bias. Conflicts between belief and archaeological evidence demonstrate that archaeo-thinking is still evolving.

The extreme postmodernist view that all interpretations have equal merit is especially dangerous when pseudo-archaeology is concerned. Outlandish interpretations about history lack the validity of traditional values and beliefs and empirical evidence. Where the Great Pyramid of Giza is concerned, should the interpretation of someone with no archaeological training and no evidence be accorded the same weight as the entire body of professional Egyptologists?

Taking postmodern thinking to its logical conclusion leads us to imagine that any interpretation of the past is equally valid. At its most extreme, we might conclude that archaeologists need not spend all their time and money (not to mention often experiencing great personal hardships) excavating ancient sites, straining to read ancient texts, and counting huge piles of potsherds. If all interpretations are equally valid, archaeologists' time might be better spent writing engaging novels about ancient Egypt than attempting the difficult work of serious archaeological research. To understand history, archaeologists require solid evidence, not eighteenth-century speculation modernized with space aliens and antigravity flying saucers. Professional archaeologists know that much of the past can be known but accept that some of it will always be lost to history. The conversations among the enslaved laborers who slid the massive stones of the Great Pyramid into place are gone forever. This loss does not mean, however, that archaeologists should cease trying to learn as much as possible about the daily lives of those individuals and the world they inhabited.

The diversity of archaeological perspectives after about 1980 has created a healthy field for archaeo-thinkers. Regardless of an archaeologist's theoretical perspective, precise methods, and analytical tools, all archaeological research requires conscious thought. Whether excavating the settlements of the earliest humans or mapping the campsites of today's homeless, all archaeologists must be clear in their arguments and logical in their suppositions. They must, as Professor Stebbing says, learn to think to some purpose. A lack of clarity of thought means that nonarchaeologists will have trouble disentangling the fantastic from the well researched. The public may not appreciate the significance of archaeological discoveries if archaeologists cannot present clear interpretations. Confining archaeological knowledge to a small circle of professionals would be a shame. The human story is too fascinating to be restricted to archaeology alone. After all, it belongs to all of us.

Continue Reading

General Thinking

Carroll, Robert Todd. 2003. *The Skeptic's Dictionary: A Collection of Strange Beliefs, Amusing Deceptions, and Dangerous Delusions.* Hoboken, NJ: John Wiley & Sons.

Feder, Kenneth L. 2006. *Frauds, Myths, and Mysteries: Science and Pseudoscience in Archaeology*. 5th ed. Boston: McGraw-Hill.

Kahneman, Daniel. 2011. *Thinking, Fast and Slow*. New York: Farrar, Straus and Giroux.

NuclearPyramid.com. http://nuclearpyramid.com/great_pyramid.php.

O'Donnell, Kevin. 2003. *Postmodernism*. Oxford: Lion Publishing.

Pierce, Charles P. 2010. *Idiot America: How Stupidity Became a Virtue in the Land of the Free*. New York: Anchor Books.

Stebbing, L. Susan. 1939. *Thinking to Some Purpose*. Harmondsworth: Penguin.

Historical Archaeo-Thinking

Adair, James. 1775. *The History of the American Indians, Particularly Those Nations Adjoining to the Mississippi, East and West Florida, Georgia, South and North Carolina, and Virginia*. London: Edward and Charles Dilly.

Atwater, Caleb. 1820. *Description of the Antiquities Discovered in the State of Ohio and Other Western States, Communicated to the President of the American Antiquarian Society*. Worcester, MA: American Antiquarian Society.

Bulwer-Lytton, Edward G. 1834. *The Last Days of Pompeii*. 3 vols. London: Richard Bentley.

Jefferson, Thomas. 1787. *Notes on the State of Virginia*. London: J. Stockdale.

Nelson, N. C. 1916. Chronology of the Tano Ruins, New Mexico. *American Anthropologist* 18:159–80.

Phillips, Philip, James A. Ford, and James B. Griffin. 1951. *Archaeological Survey in the Lower Mississippi Alluvial Valley, 1940–1947*. Cambridge, MA: Peabody Museum, Harvard University. Reprinted in 2003 by the University of Alabama Press, Tuscaloosa.

Spier, Leslie. 1917. *An Outline for a Chronology of Zuñi Ruins*. Anthropological Papers of the American Museum of Natural History, vol. 18, pt. 3. New York: American Museum of Natural History.

Squier, Ephraim G., and Edwin H. Davis. 1848. *Ancient Monuments of the Mississippi Valley: Comprising the Results of Extensive Original Surveys and Explorations*. Washington, DC: Smithsonian Institution.

Taylor, Walter W. 1948. *A Study of Archaeology*. Memoir 69. Washington, DC: American Anthropological Association.

Thomas, Cyrus. 1887. *Work in Mound Exploration of the Bureau of Ethnology*. Washington, DC: Government Printing Office.

It All Seems So Sciencey   **2**
Archaeology, Science, and History

IF TELEVISION PROGRAMMING AND ONLINE VIDEO viewing is any
judge, we may reasonably conclude that millions of people are interested in what archaeology reveals about human history. Whether on
land or under the sea, the process of discovery makes archaeology inherently intriguing. Even the most highly trained, experienced archaeologist
never knows what the next scoop of earth will reveal, and, like everyone
else, professional archaeologists enjoy the thrill of discovery.

The almost infinite diversity contained in the human story gives archaeology its special appeal. Archaeologists explore the entire span of human history, extending from Day 1 to yesterday. On any given day, a team
of archaeologists can be found somewhere in the world sifting through the
earth searching for lost information about the lives of our human ancestors. Archaeologists may be in France entering a cave once inhabited by a
family of Neanderthals, and only a few miles away another team might be
measuring a cement bunker used by German soldiers during World War
II. Others may be studying ancient DNA in Ethiopia, the distribution of
gravestones in a seventeenth-century English cemetery, or the trash deposits of a twenty-first-century Brazilian landfill. The diversity of subjects
demonstrates archaeology's limitless possibilities. Each new research project promises endless new discoveries.

Despite the great variety in possible topics, all archaeologists are united
by one common element: the way they address the questions they want answered. Unlike the nuclear proponent mentioned in chapter 1, professional
archaeologists must develop questions that can be evaluated with tangible
evidence. They cannot simply proclaim an interpretation and expect other

archaeologists to accept it without proof. Untrained amateur interpret- ers—pseudo-archaeologists—are free to propound any ideas they wish. As nonprofessional hobbyists not committed to the same rules of evidence and research as professional excavators, they have complete freedom to create any interpretation they can imagine. Like the armchair-bound archaeologists of centuries ago, pseudo-archaeologists do not conduct excavations (at least not legally, that is). Their interpretations thus typically rest on supposition, wishful thinking, and speculation. Professional archaeologists have the same freedom of expression but with far greater cost to their careers and reputations if they engage in wild speculation. A professor of archaeology who concludes that the Great Pyramid really *was* a nuclear facility, without substantial evidence, may suffer professionally and lose the respect of colleagues. Unlike pseudo- archaeologists, professionals are held to high scientific standards.

How Do Archaeologists Use Science and History to Think?

Individual archaeologists use science in different ways. Some conduct highly scientific research using sophisticated equipment, complex chemi- cal testing, and multivariate statistics. Archaeologists seeking to recover the residues of fats and oils from ancient clay pots or attempting to obtain DNA samples from ancient bones share a close relationship with chemists and physicists. Other archaeologists may use high-tech methods of digital mapping, GIS, and complex algorithms to map site locations and to puzzle out how past cultures chose their settlement locations. These archaeolo- gists are perfectly at home collaborating with statisticians, NASA scientists, and geologists. Many of them may even refer to themselves as archaeo- logical scientists. In other cases, an archaeologist's use of science may be much more difficult to identify. Archaeologists interested in understand- ing the relationships between consumer objects and gender relations at a nineteenth-century Chinese mining camp in California may not appear to rely on science at all. These archaeologists may place more emphasis on written histories, personal stories and memories, old maps, and other sources of information that are far removed from the chemist's lab. Many archaeologists feel more at home in the social sciences than in the hard sciences, and others think of themselves as historians. Despite the variation among archaeologists, it would be incorrect to conclude that any archae- ologist is divorced from the world of the archaeological scientist who has found remains requiring chemical analysis. All archaeologists use scientific thinking to some degree.

As you saw in the first chapter, the amount of scientific thinking may vary from person to person. At the most basic level, all archaeologists use science when they rely on systematic concepts of observation, measurement, and evaluation. Even extreme postmodernists, when they excavate, must rely on the same scientifically based field methods as the most ardent hypothesis-testing, process-oriented archaeologist.

Fieldwork, when archaeologists collect their most unique information, is an easy place to see the role of science in archaeological research. Systematic excavation involves laying out standardized excavation grids, writing detailed notes, taking photographs, drafting scale drawings and maps, and recording careful vertical and horizontal measurements. The care taken to document every step in the process is a necessary feature that sets professional archaeologists apart from nonprofessional, pseudo-archaeologists. Trained professionals conduct a great deal of research and planning before they ever arrive in the field to excavate. Unplanned digging is simply looting, and no professional archaeologist wants to be perceived as a looter. Archaeologists know their efforts will be wasted if they fail to be as careful as possible. Little useful information will come from a sloppy, poorly documented field project.

Professional archaeologists engage in a systematic research process that involves first locating sites and then carefully planning their excavation. This process may take years of background research and field surveying. This preliminary legwork is necessary because archaeologists realize that excavation destroys. The act of turning over soil layers and disturbing the remains within them demolishes the excavated part of the site forever. Archaeologist Philip Barker once observed that excavation, no matter how carefully performed and diligently recorded, "is like cutting pieces out of a hitherto unexamined manuscript, transcribing the fragments, and then destroying them." He added that any self-respecting historian would be enraged by this act, even though archaeologists accept it as a valid research method. Knowing the destructive power of excavation, professional archaeologists undertake it with extreme caution. They know that fieldwork involves just as much paperwork as excavation.

Many people think that archaeology is only about finding artifacts. Artifacts are a central piece of the cultural and historical puzzles to be sure, but they constitute only one kind of evidence. Other evidence includes the location of artifacts relative to one another both vertically and horizontally as well as to all those things—hearths, storage pits, postholes, and housing remains—that cannot be removed from the ground and taken into the archaeologist's laboratory. Archaeologists can measure and record these features only as they appear in the soil. Some of the more stable re-mains—adobe house walls and brick hearths—can be left in place, but the more fragile features—postholes and storage pits—are lost forever when excavated.

All archaeologists make interpretations once they return from the field. The laboratory is where they begin to evaluate their findings and assess the initial impressions they formed while excavating. This intellectual process also relies on science to some degree because it is here that the second phase of archaeo-thinking emerges. The real work of interpretation begins after the specimens have been washed, entered into a database, photo-graphed, and closely examined and once the collection of maps, drawings, and photographs have been analyzed. How archaeologists do this work is the heart and soul of archaeo-thinking. In its essence, it merges science and the humanities, craft and art.

SEARCHing

In their clever book *How to Think about Weird Things*, Theodore Schick and Lewis Vaughn present a research program they call SEARCH. Al-though not created with archaeology in mind, this formula provides an excellent way to envision the basic, overall structure of archaeo-thinking. The acronym SEARCH stands for the various steps of the process, which Schick and Lewis present as follows:

1. State the claim.
2. Examine the Evidence for the claim.
3. Consider Alternative claims.
4. Rate, according to the Criteria of adequacy, each Hypothesis [claim].

Before exploring the process itself, the obvious question is, What are hy-potheses, and do all archaeologists use them?

Hypotheses can be tricky, sciencey-sounding things, but we can think of them simply as questions about something. Schick and Vaughn use "hypothesis" and "claim" interchangeably, and their usage helps explain that a hypothesis is a statement that can be answered with research. All scientists address hypotheses (claims) regardless of their field of inquiry, and this includes archaeologists, even those who might not view their research as particularly scientific.

SEARCH is one way of seeking resolution to claims. Another way to say this is, How does anyone know that a claim has merit?

Thinking back to the claim presented in chapter 1—that the Great Pyramid was used as a nuclear facility—we could state this claim: "The Great Pyramid was used as a nuclear energy generator." We could also state the claim as a question: "Was the Great Pyramid used to create nuclear energy?" Either way, we have now stated a claim we would like to have answered with evidence.

Step 1: State the Claim

The first element of SEARCH is simply to state the claim. This seems obvious, but the point is that the claim must be made explicit and clear so that everyone understands what is being investigated. Archaeological research is often like opening one door to reveal two more, which in turn leads to another two and so forth. As a result, researchers must state the exact claim they wish to address so that the goal of their research is clear.

A claim, whatever it is, must be answerable with verifiable evidence. Hypotheses that cannot be addressed have no place in the process. For example, the claim "It takes 135 gremlins to fill up a VW Beetle" is not good because its validity cannot be tested with evidence. We are unlikely to find even one gremlin that we can entice into the Beetle. (If we could locate just one, we could measure its size, shape, and mass and extrapolate from there. Once we knew the interior space of a Beetle, we'd then have a pretty good idea whether our claim was accurate. But alas, no gremlin, no test!) The claim "Zombies will appear at midnight tonight on the quad" is a valid (though undesirable) question because we can actually test it. We can camp out and wait to see whether any of the undead shows up at the stroke of 12. This claim may not be a serious one, but it can be addressed with tangible evidence.

Step 2: Examine the Evidence

The problem behind our use of gremlins relates to the second element of the SEARCH protocol. This step requires that we examine the evidence for the claim. For gremlins, we have no physical (empirical) evidence for their existence. We can only imagine the average size of one, but what *I* imagine may be completely different from what *you* may imagine. We'd both be right, and no one could prove us wrong. We can be proven wrong only when someone captures a gremlin and measures it. Until this happens (which is incredibly unlikely), our claims cannot be evaluated or even really criticized because they spring only from our imaginations. They are merely speculative.

The claim that the Great Pyramid was used as a nuclear facility includes evidence that can be evaluated. Europeans first learned about the Egyptian pyramids through the works of French, German, and English tourists who began to write about them in the sixteenth century. The first actual European investigation of the Great Pyramid occurred in 1798 when Napoleon's scholar-soldiers studied it during the French invasion of Egypt (figure 2.1).

Archaeologists have been exploring Giza ever since. Throughout all of this time, not a single piece of evidence has been found that even remotely suggests that the Great Pyramid created nuclear materials. Instead, archaeologists have only found evidence that reinforces the most obvious conclusion: that ancient Egyptians built this ancient Egyptian monument. So, under the second step of the SEARCH process, we can consider the evidence for the nuclear interpretation. The undeniable conclusion is that no evidence exists. The nuclear interpretation is mere fantasy. It's very interesting, but it's simply wishful thinking. Realistically, we are left with the interpretations of professional Egyptologists who have spent lifetimes studying every facet of ancient Egyptian life using tangible evidence.

Figure 2.1.   Napoleon's army at the Great Pyramid. From *Description de l'Égypte, ou recueil des observations et des recherches qui ont été faites en Égypte pendant l'expédition de l'armée française* (Paris: Imprímerie imériale, 1822).

Given the real mysteries surrounding the pyramid, we should not be surprised that professional archaeologists disagree about some interpretations. Detailed archaeological studies, such as John Romer's *The Great Pyramid*, illustrate the complexities present within the pyramid's architecture. Respectable scholars have disagreed about something as basic as the size of the pyramid! For example, in the early 1880s, the famed British archaeologist William Flinders Petrie discovered that earlier surveyors had made a series of errors when measuring the pyramid's base. To correct their mistakes, he provided new measurements. The problem is that the measurement depends on where one places the measuring tape and what he or she considers to be the actual base. The rock faces are not as smooth as we might suppose, so some variation between measurements is inevitable. Archaeologists wishing to understand the Great Pyramid's inner architecture have been hampered by the sheer size of the structure and the difficulty of accurately measuring its many shafts and chambers. Thus, something as basic as measurement can be a subject of considerable debate among professional archaeologists, even though measurement, by its very nature, is an element of careful scientific procedure.

When examining the evidence for a claim, it is important to ignore wishful thinking, belief, faith, and intuition. We may secretly wish zombies would visit the quad at midnight, but wishing will not make them appear. Our belief in the existence of the walking undead is discounted by the lack of tangible evidence.

Millions of people around the world believe that space aliens are piloting UFOs to our planet. This belief has sponsored a huge commercial industry, but until a spaceship lands or crashes on Earth (and is retrieved), the existence of space aliens must remain only wishful thinking (or dreadful thinking if you think they might be up to no good).

Step 3: Consider Alternative Claims

Step 3 of the SEARCH process asks us to consider alternative claims. This means that before we can accept one claim as true, we must think about and evaluate others. Perhaps an alternative claim makes more sense than the one we originally selected. To decide between them, we must compare the evidence for each of them.

To demonstrate the process, let's use this claim: space aliens are visiting Earth in a number of fast-moving vehicles we collectively term UFOs (this is Step 1, stating the claim). When we examine the evidence (Step 2), we learn the following:

- Millions of people believe in UFOs.
- Millions of people have seen lights in the sky they cannot explain as airplanes, blimps, stars, weather balloons, and other Earth-made things.
- Hundreds of people claim to have been abducted by aliens, and many of them have told believable stories of their experiences.
- A number of television programs and online videos show pictures of UFOs, and organizations like the Mutual UFO Network keep track of their appearances throughout the world.
- Both professional and amateur pilots have reported seeing strange things in the sky.
- Many nations' air forces have been unable to explain a large number of sightings. The U.S. Air Force even had a full-blown investigation called Project Bluebook to investigate whether UFOs are real, and even they could not always provide credible interpretations.

These factors have convinced millions of people around the world that visitors from far-distant planets are among us and that they have traveled here in otherworldly aircraft using advanced technologies completely unknown to us. Some people even believe that the U.S. government has been reverse engineering the aliens' technology at Nevada's Area 51, using parts from crashed flying saucers.

A number of scientists and skeptics have presented several alternative hypotheses to account for what people are seeing in the skies. One of the most prominent is that people are really witnessing the testing of secret military aircraft. Many UFO sightings occur near airports and military bases. Believers and Ufologists (people who specialize in studying the phenomenon) say the locations of the sighting are not accidental; they claim that aliens are checking out the state of our aircraft. This is one conclusion, but might the locations of the sightings simply have something to do with human flight?

Let's consider some evidence that will help us evaluate the alternative claim. In a report published in the United Kingdom's *Guardian* newspaper in April 2010, the U.S. Defense Advanced Research Projects Agency oversaw the flight of a prototype aircraft named the Falcon Hypersonic Technology Vehicle, or HTV-2, at Vandenberg Air Force Base in California. The amazing thing about the test flight was that the HTV-2 reached Mach 20, or about 13,000 miles per hour, for about three minutes. If this plane could hold this speed constant, it could travel the 10,500 miles between London, England, and Sydney, Australia, in less than an hour! (The current flight time by regular airplane is about 23 hours.) This speed is remarkable because the fastest aircraft in the world is the Lockheed SR-71 Blackbird. It can reach a top speed of 2,193 miles per hour. This is fast but nowhere near the speed of the HTV-2. The two fastest military fighter planes are said to be the Lockheed Martin F-22 Raptor (with a top speed of 1,498 miles per hour) and the Russian-built Sukhoi T-50 PAK FA Stealth Fighter (with a top speed of between 1,300 and 1,560 miles per hour). These high speeds are significant because many UFO spotters have reported that they've never seen anything move as fast as the UFO they observed.

Another factor we must consider is how long it would take space aliens to reach the Earth. As you might expect, physicists disagree about this because much of it rests on speculation. Nonetheless, a few truths based on the laws of physics make it possible to propose some fairly reliable ideas.

Interstellar travel, whether by Earthlings or aliens, is constrained by distance, time, and power. Scientists know that the speed of light in a vacuum is constant at about 1 billion miles per hour. Einstein famously demonstrated that space and time are relative (hence the theory of relativity). This means that as people travel faster in space, time slows down and space becomes shorter. Mass also increases. The implications for space travel, as science writer Michael White observes in *Weird Science*, is that a person traveling at the speed of light would experience three things: "time would slow to nothing, he would shrink to nothing, and his mass would be infinite!" Thus, aliens leaving their home planet and traveling 50 light-years to Earth at a speed of 95 percent the speed of light would need about 52.5 years to reach Earth. But, because time slows down, the alien crew would age only about 15 years. Science fiction buffs know what this means. The entire trip to Earth and back would take over 100 years for the people on the home planet, but the travelers would have aged only about 30 years. On their arrival, they would find their friends and relatives dead or very old, their grandchildren would be older than them, they might find a new political or economic system, and so forth; the possibilities are endless.

Given the constraints of physics, some people have proposed that space aliens may have acted similar to the ancient Polynesians who traveled thousands of miles to colonize the entire South Pacific. To accomplish this monumental feat, the Polynesians sailed their canoes from island to island rather than undertaking one long-distance trek. Adopting an island-hopping method, aliens could have planet-hopped using some sort of super-advanced spacecraft. But even with advanced technology, they need to create colonies on each planet they visited and prepare for the next hop (as the Polynesians did). On reaching the next planet, they would have to begin the process all over again.

Realizing that interstellar voyaging has infinitely longer distances be-tween planets than Pacific sailing, we are justified in asking just how long planet-hopping would take. The amount of required fuel would be huge, even using the Polynesians' method. Physicists estimate that a spaceship traveling at only 10 percent of the speed of light would require about 15 times its mass in fuel. Long-distance space travel would require extremely large ships. Even Erich von Däniken, the hotel manager who started the ancient astronaut craze with his completely speculative *Chariots of the Gods?*, admits that a space-traveling ship would have to be the size of a modern ocean liner and have a payload of 200 tons (with half of it being dedicated to fuel alone). Given the sheer size requirements and the amount of energy required, planet-hopping aliens would have to establish produc-tion facilities on each of their colonized planets to replenish the fuel they would need to reach the next planet. Without planet-hopping, the amount of fuel needed to travel huge distances would make any trip unrealistic.

Knowing all this, let's go back to our two claims about UFOs. Our main hypothesis is that space aliens visit the Earth on a regular basis and that people see them and call their spaceships UFOs. Our alternative hy-pothesis is that UFOs are misrecognized, top-secret planes undergoing testing near airports and other governmental facilities. According to Step 4 of the SEARCH protocol, our job now is to evaluate each claim and de-cide which one makes more sense than the other based on what evidence we can amass.

The easiest approach is simply to compare the kinds of evidence pre-sented for each claim. For the alien claim, most of the evidence is based on anecdotes, or what scientists term "testimonial evidence."

There is nothing inherently wrong with testimonies, and archaeologists use them all the time. An archaeologist excavating a farmhouse dating to within living memory may choose to speak with former residents to obtain unique insights about life on the farm. Men and women who once lived on the property can tell stories about their pastimes, they can explain how the furniture was arranged in the house, they can talk about what they ate, and they can relate what they did in the yard areas. This information may exist only in their memories, never having been written down. Historian Carl Becker famously referred to this evidence as "history people carry around in their heads."

Even archaeologists studying history before the presence of writing may ask local residents about their activities at a particular place, what they re-member about artifacts they may have seen in the soil or in their neighbors' collections, and whether they know any local people knowledgeable about

local history and archaeology. When archaeologists use this kind of information, they realize that people's memories can be faulty. People remember
things selectively, forget, misrepresent, and get confused. As a result, anecdotes, however interesting they may be, constitute often-useful but also potentially unreliable evidence. If a 95-year-old former resident of a farmhouse
tells you that she had cable television in 1950 and that she remembers watching YouTube as a child, you can be pretty certain her recollections have
little value. The reliability of verbal evidence decreases when something like
UFOs are the subject because verification is impossible.

Step 4: Rate Each Claim

In Step 4 of the SEARCH formula, Schick and Vaughn introduce what they
term "the criteria of adequacy." These criteria help us evaluate the strength
of the competing claims, meaning that we don't have to make decisions
based on our feelings, what we might wish to be true, or our speculations.

The criteria of adequacy has five elements:

1. Testability
2. Fruitfulness
3. Scope
4. Simplicity
5. Conservatism

After an investigator has worked through the five criteria, he or she should
have a good understanding of whether a claim makes sense.

The first criterion, testability, is exactly what it sounds like: can someone figure out a way to determine whether a claim can be evaluated by
testing? If it cannot be tested (and using methods that others can copy),
then the claim is worthless. This doesn't mean that it's untrue, however;
it simply means that it has no value as a verifiable claim. Something that
cannot be tested usually falls under the heading of belief.

Of the two competing claims about UFOs, only the second one can
be tested. If the military would allow it, we could arrange to have a top-
secret, supersonic plane fly over two neighborhoods. The first neighborhood would be one in which the residents recently said they saw a UFO;
the second neighborhood would be one that has not witnessed a UFO
sighting. After the flights, we could ask the residents what they saw, and
then we could tabulate how many thought they saw a UFO. We must
remember, though, that even the residents who saw the first sighting could

say that what they saw during the test did not resemble "their" UFO. They may have seen a different prototype during their first sighting, the weather could have been different, their allergies may have made their eyesight fuzzy, and so forth. We could test the claim that the witnessed UFO was really the test flight of a super-secret Earth-bound aircraft, but we would still have several additional factors to consider.

The claim about UFOs being piloted by aliens, however, is untestable. To demonstrate this, let's turn to popular television. Their boasts to the contrary, "investigative" programs cannot "unmask the truth" about UFOs. The videos they show are usually blurred and shaky. Tests of the "best" videos by skilled technicians either are inconclusive or reveal hoaxes. No currently available video—no matter how mysterious it may seem—has been proven to provide direct evidence for alien visitation.

The second criterion of adequacy, fruitfulness, refers to what a claim can do for us; in other words, can it provide new ideas and insights and create new questions that can be asked and tested? As Schick and Vaughn point out, most claims related to the paranormal, UFOs, and other mysterious phenomena seldom expand inquiry into new topics. One door does not lead to two new doors because the first door is never really opened. As a result, claims about mysterious phenomena have little or no fruitfulness. Ufologists, because they have only the weakest of evidence, simply keep asking the same questions over and over again:

- Are space aliens real, and are they visiting Earth?
- When did they first arrive?
- What do they look like?
- What do they want here?

UFO chasers cannot progress beyond this point because they have no concrete evidence to support their views; they have only anecdotes, jumpy videos, and a handful of still photographs. On the other hand, the alternative idea about UFOs being airplanes made by Earth-bound humans can lead to other avenues of investigation. If we were allowed to witness a secret test, we could think of a number of questions to ask. We'd probably want to know about the effects that pilots suffer at high speeds, the kind of fuel and its rate of depletion, who makes the engines and what kind they are, and a hundred other questions, all of which could be answered either by knowledgeable scientists or our own research. The alternative claim therefore has a high degree of fruitfulness because it leads to a host of other questions.

The third criterion is scope, which refers to how many other phenomena a claim can explain. A rule of thumb among scientists is that the more a claim explains, the likelier it is to be true. If we conclude that the UFO sightings are military aircraft, we could explain why so many are seen near airports, why Area 51 and other governmental research facilities have tight security, why the air force never provides information, and why the test pilots who fly them take their knowledge to the grave. The scope of the UFOs = space aliens claim is extremely narrow because it leads nowhere. Nothing is explained.

Simplicity is the fourth criteria of adequacy. This criterion relies on another scientific rule of thumb: that the simplest claims tend to be correct, with "simple" referring to the number of assumptions that must be made. Scientists usually refer to this as "Occam's Razor" in honor of William of Occam, a medieval English friar who often used the idea in his philosophical arguments. The metaphor of the razor helps us imagine shaving off as many assumptions from our claim as possible.

The number of assumptions needed to accept the idea that UFOs are piloted by space aliens is astronomical, beginning with the two most obvious ones: that space aliens exist and that they wish to visit us Earthlings. From this follows innumerable additional assumptions concerning the nature of their fuel, the design of their engines, their advanced technology, the distances they've traveled, and how their bodies are able to withstand the extremely high speeds needed for space travel. And these are just a few of the assumptions we must make. Thinking about the aliens' role in building the Great Pyramid, we would have to ask this simple question: why would aliens travel all this way in super-high-tech spaceships just to build a simple pyramid in the middle of the Egyptian desert? Why not build something as high-tech as their ships? Why would they build a nuclear plant since they obviously had a more advanced form of energy? We would have to overlook such obvious questions and simply accept the assumption that space aliens like traveling vast distances to build pyramid-shaped nuclear facilities in deserts (while leaving no other trace of their presence).

One of the most interesting assumptions that we'd have to make about the physical evidence presented in the UFO videos is that psychologists are wrong about the "autokinetic effect." This is a physical phenomenon whereby people think a stationary light is moving when they see it against a dark background. Involuntary movements of the eye, which occur even when we hold our heads perfectly still, convince us that the light is moving when it's not. In the early twentieth century, psychologist Joseph Peterson set up an experiment to prove the existence of the effect. In the course of his testing, he discovered two interesting things that help us understand peoples' strong belief in UFOs: first, that because the autokinetic effect frightens some people, they immediately conclude that what they see must be supernatural or otherworldly, and, second, that the lights appear to move even when the subjects of the experiment know the lights are completely stationary. We can easily see how the autokinetic effect could figure into some claims about UFO sightings.

The final criterion of adequacy is conservatism, which refers to how well a claim conforms to what we already know. In this instance, rather than simply listing the alternative claims as we did in Step 3, here we must assign relative weights to each competing claim. Here the process is simple because we have only two claims. Based on what I have presented, is it more likely that UFOs are

a. visitations by space aliens or
b. secret airplanes being tested by governmental agencies?

The evidence leads us to accept the alternative hypothesis (b) as most likely based on everything we know and on the simplicity of the claim. We make fewer assumptions when we accept that governmental agencies are probably testing futuristic aircraft over our heads. The alternative claim has much greater weight than the claim about space aliens.

We can accept the alternative claim even though millions of people around the world continue to believe that space aliens are visiting Earth. This idea acquired an archaeological dimension when von Däniken revealed his claim about ancient astronauts in the late 1960s. Since then, he and others have developed a thriving industry by claiming that the greatest archaeological sites in the world, including the Great Pyramid, are the product of alien technology rather than tangible proof of the intelligence and creativity of our human ancestors. As archaeologist Kenneth Feder states in "Help! I'm Being Followed by Ancient Aliens!," not only has no archaeological evidence ever been found for aliens—no ray guns, no phasers, no antigravity machines—but we simply don't need to imagine ancient spacemen (and women, I presume) either building a pyramid in the Egyptian desert or teaching the Egyptians how to build it. The very real archaeological mysteries remaining to be solved should be enough to keep us interested without having to invent untestable, wild claims.

Plausibility

We must understand one more thing. The nature of hypothetical claims is such that we can never completely prove them, especially in archaeology.

All we can do is to tend to accept them. Why? Because we can never be 100 percent certain that we've collected all the evidence, even for UFOs. The job of all researchers—physicists, biologists, archaeologists, historians—is to acquire knowledge about our world. Whereas physical scientists can absolutely prove a claim with evidence, archaeologists and historians always work with partial evidence. As a result, archaeologists usually speak in terms of *probability* or *plausibility* rather than 100 percent certainty.

In *Evidence Explained*, Elizabeth Shown Mills observes that scholars engaged in historical research usually use certain words to signify their lack of complete certainty. Ranging from least likelihood to most, the telltale words are "perhaps" (an idea is plausible but untested), "apparently" (a scholar has formed an impression based on experience but has not tested the idea), "likely" (the weight of evidence tilts toward the assertion), "possibly" (good evidence exists, but the claim is not yet proved), and "probably" (the assertion is more likely than not based on the evidence at hand). All archaeologists use these terms, though perhaps not with the same levels of meaning as Mills suggests. In any case, such common terms indicate that no one alive today can know the past with certainty, Mills's highest level of confidence. Students reading the works of archaeologists should be on the lookout for these terms.

The need to understand plausibility is especially important for archaeologists (and others who study history) because the whole truth about the past can never be known in its entirety (see chapter 3). The past is gone, and all of its secrets will never be revealed. No one can re-create history in every detail. Going back to SEARCH, then, we can ask, What is the most plausible interpretation based on the evidence we have at hand right now? And "now" is key because knowledge increases with every new investigation or, in the case of archaeology, with each new excavation and reanalysis.

Archaeologists do not make the mistake of thinking they know everything; they know that they are constrained by the current state of their discipline's knowledge and that knowledge grows as more studies are completed. For example, only a few years ago, the current advances in understanding human genetics were unimaginable. It would have been wrong in 1950 to think that medical researchers knew everything about the human body. Stopping their research would have been a horrible idea because what we have learned in the interim has been astronomical.

In terms of plausibility, we must decide—based on our current knowledge—that it is much more likely that UFOs are secret aircraft rather than alien-powered spaceships. But can we completely discount the claim that some UFOs are space aliens? Surprisingly, not entirely.

Although extremely unlikely, it remains remotely possible that one day a spaceship may crash in broad daylight in New York City and be witnessed by hundreds of people (before the mysterious men in black can remove it!). The probability of this event ever occurring is infinitesimally small, but it remains possible. Astronomers agree that the huge number of galaxies and planets in the universe make it statistically possible for life to exist beyond Earth. Despite this conclusion, significant questions remain as to what these life forms may be like and whether they could (or would) ever wish to visit us. The possibility of an alien visit is so tiny as to be virtually impossible, but no one can see into the future. What is not plausible is that ancient space aliens built the Great Pyramid, that they erected England's Stonehenge, or that they are responsible for Peru's Nasca lines (figure 2.2). It is pure fantasy to think they built these monuments.

The Exeter Mystery

I have purposefully kept my UFO example simple to make it easier to understand the basics of the SEARCH formula. It always helps, however, to present a real incident to explain how the belief in UFOs and space aliens can rest alongside the scientific search for more plausible explanations. A real case, called the "Exeter Incident," demonstrates how long it can take for a realistic interpretation to emerge from the world of fantasy.

Just after midnight on September 3, 1965, in Exeter, New Hampshire, a police officer was driving along a road when he encountered a woman parked on the shoulder. When he stopped to investigate, he found the driver agitated and excited. She told him she had been followed for several miles by a flying object with red flashing lights. She pointed toward the horizon, where both she and the policeman saw a bright light. Not having an explanation but seeing no danger, the cop told her there was nothing to worry about and left. About two hours later, however, a visibly shaken teenager arrived at the Exeter police station. He reported that while hitchhiking toward home, he had seen a huge ship in the sky. He signed a statement and agreed to accompany an officer to the site. On arriving in the area of the sighting, the officer also saw the object and reported that it had five bright, red lights. Over the next several weeks, over 60 witnesses filed similar reports about strange lights in the sky, and in February 1966, a story even appeared in *Look*, a popular biweekly magazine read by millions of Americans. Thus was born the Exeter Incident.

Figure 2.2.   A set of Paracas and Nasca geoglyphs and lines (200 BCE–600 CE) called the "Reloj Solar" in Palpa, Peru. Trapezoidal lines of the Nasca culture intersect an earlier geometric spiraling labyrinth inscribed on the flat surface of the Sacramento Ridge above the Palpa Valley. Photo by Brendan J. M. Weaver. Director, Proyecto Arqueológico Haciendas de Nasca. Used by permission.

True believers in the connection between strange lights in the sky and advanced space travelers quickly transformed the incident into a "close encounter of the first kind." It quickly entered UFO folklore, where it has prominently remained ever since.

As you may expect, a number of people offered alternative ideas about what the people may actually have seen. Some of these claims are that the lights were the following:

- Stars or planets
- The glare of landing lights from aircraft going into nearby Pease Air Force Base, a Strategic Air Command and NORAD base
- Part of an air force operation
- An advertising plane with a flying billboard
- The corona from power lines
- A prankster with a lighted kite

Skeptics presented each of these alternative interpretations, but none were ever tested. As a result, for 40 years the Exeter Incident has remained an important fixture within Ufology. It took two researchers, James McGaha and Joe Nickell, to provide the most likely alternative interpretation of what the people in New Hampshire had witnessed.

McGaha, a former military pilot, realized that the light sequence the people reported seeing perfectly matched the lights on a U.S. Air Force KC-97 refueling plane. These planes not only had a row of five red, flashing lights mounted on their fuselages but also were based at Pease Air Force Base in the 1960s. When a plane was to be refueled in the air, a very delicate operation at night, the KC-97 pilot would turn on the lights to tell the pilot in the other plane that the fuel boom had been lowered. As the second pilot approached, the KC-97 pilot would dim the sequencing lights so as not to blind the approaching pilot. This operation would undoubtedly look strange to an observer on the ground, especially at night by someone unfamiliar with the process (as most people would be).

Most serious UFO researchers now regard this famous "cold case" as closed. The incident clearly demonstrates the importance of considering alternative interpretations, even if it takes years of thinking. Archaeologists understand the time it often takes to acquire enough evidence to be able to propose plausible claims about long-dead civilizations.

The Ongoing Tussle between Evidence and Perspective

Claims are a dry subject that seems devoid of human emotion. Perhaps in learning about the SEARCH formula and the criteria of adequacy, you pictured serious scientists in white lab coats toiling away in those ultra-clean, white rooms often depicted in science fiction movies (the ones from which the aliens usually escape). In truth, though, a great deal of a person's education and experience goes into the creation of claims and the decisions made about plausibility. This is where the art of archaeological interpretation comes into view.

In a perfectly regimented world, the process of deciding between competing claims would be as straightforward as knowing that water boils at 212°F—and just about as interesting. Thankfully, archaeology—because human cultures are its subject matter—involves a process of discovery and interpretation that is anything but humdrum. Each researcher, even when strictly adhering to the SEARCH method, interjects his or her ideas, passions, and interests into the process. And once human personality is introduced, many different perspectives can result, and great controversies over interpretation can occur.

In *Reading Matter*, Arthur Berger presents a perfect example of how one's professional discipline may shape one's interpretations. In a hypothetical scenario, he envisions six scholars sitting in their individual offices in the same building. Each of them has a window that looks down on a central courtyard. In the courtyard is a picnic table with a McDonald's hamburger, a package of French fries, and a milkshake on it. The scholars are a semiotician (someone who studies symbols and their meanings), a psychoanalytic psychologist, a cultural anthropologist, a historian, a sociologist, and a political scientist. Each scholar, because of his or her perspectives, educational training, and personality, interprets the objects on the table differently.

The semiotician perceives the objects as a series of symbols. To her, they symbolize America, the efficiency of mass production, and the standardization of food preparation. She understands that the Golden Arches printed on the wrapping, the cup, and the bag as some of the most recognizable symbols throughout the world. In a broad way, the symbol may represent the United States and its global economic reach.

The psychologist, on the other hand, sees the objects as representing the desire for instant gratification and depersonalization. The hamburgers, fries, and milkshakes, wherever consumed in the world, all look and taste alike. A McDonald's hamburger in Dublin, Ireland, tastes just like one in St. Louis, Missouri. Individual consumers cannot decide whether they'd like their hamburger cooked a little longer or have their fries cooked in an exotic kind of oil. When you go to McDonald's, you get what everyone else gets (with some minor variation perhaps).

The historian immediately sees the objects on the table in terms of the history of corporations and how twentieth-century U.S. corporations became multinationals following World War II. He also envisions how the presentation of the food changed American eating and driving habits because the first McDonald's did not have tables inside them. He might also think about the ways the restaurants are linked to the development of American car culture and the development of outlying suburbs.

The cultural anthropologist perceives the objects as parts of a ritual. During the early years of the company, teenagers had to go into the restaurant and order their food from a counter. Receiving their order, they had to leave because of the lack of tables. They ate their meals in their cars and drove around as they did so. The anthropologist interprets this behavior as part of a mating ritual, with the site of the restaurant being a ritualized place where eligible partners can meet without their parents being present.

The sociologist thinks about how people, perhaps especially young people, use such objects to feel part of a group and how fast-food restaurants have become places where people of all ages meet and socialize. She might also consider how places like McDonald's have become especially important to disadvantaged families as relatively inexpensive places to eat and how difficult it may be for poor people to escape the low-wage service jobs that fast-food restaurants offer.

The political scientist perceives the food on the table as examples of how corporations have become extremely powerful in the Western world and how they are rapidly moving into the Global South. He may see McDonald's as the worst example of globalization because it exploits its workforce while it spreads the poor American diet to the rest of the world.

What is notable about Berger's scenario is that each of the scholars uses the exact same pieces of material culture—a hamburger, some fries, and a milkshake—to frame their interpretations. The addition of more scholars—perhaps an architect, a neuroscientist, a marketing professor, and a feminist—would add to the diversity of interpretations. What is interesting, though, is that none of them would be incorrect. Their perspectives are simply different because they have examined the objects from a different angle. It is here, then, that we see the challenge of analysis despite the power of the SEARCH protocol. Individuals simply have different ways of perceiving the world around them.

Instead of having scholars from different disciplines looking down at a picnic table, what would happen if six archaeologists examined a new collection of artifacts at a museum? What if the archaeologists included a Marxist, a feminist, an ecologist, a Darwinian, a critical theorist, and a network analyst? Archaeologists holding each perspective are active today. Each of these archaeologists, just like Berger's group of scholars in the office building, can examine the same pieces of material culture and devise different interpretations. The differences of opinion developing as a result of diverse interpretations keep archaeology vibrant and interesting.

One of the key features of serious scholarship, especially in a discipline like archaeology, is that ideas, concepts, and interpretations change as more information is gathered and as new perspectives emerge. Some of the perspectives that develop derive directly from the concerns of society rather than specifically from scientific inquiry. For example, the archaeology of American enslavement arose in the late 1960s in direct response to the civil rights movement and the growing interest in ethnic pride. When archaeologists excavated plantation sites before the 1960s, their focus was usually on the mansion and its white, wealthy residents. The civil rights and ethnic pride movements made archaeologists wonder what life had been like where most plantation residents lived: in the cabins of the enslaved. Archaeologists thus began to excavate cabin remains to satisfy their curiosity, and today a large number of historical archaeologists throughout the Americas concentrate their efforts on the archaeology of the African Diaspora. The civil rights movement had brought the issue of racial discrimination to the forefront of national thinking. Minority groups, held down and ignored, voiced their concerns about many social issues, one of which being an unfair separation from their histories. Native Americans and African Americans, as well as others, demanded to have a say in how their histories were portrayed. At the same time, scholars in many academic disciplines had started to question their own goals, motivations, and perspectives as they pertained to the world's minorities. Anthropologists, historians, geographers, and others began to address racial inequality and to modify their curricula and research to be more inclusive. This group also included archaeologists. In fact, an interesting case study of perception and archaeological interpretation emerged during this era of initial research into the living conditions of people of African heritage in the New World.

The Changing Nature of Coarse, Low-Fired Earthenware

In the late 1960s, as archaeologists excavated an increasing number of colonial sites in Virginia, they noticed that many of the artifacts they discovered were made in the general shape of English cups, bowls, and saucers but that, unlike British ceramics, their potters had made them from local clays, left them unglazed, and fired them at fairly low temperatures. These vessels looked crude compared with the white-bodied, glazed ceramics imported from England.

Archaeologists had no evidence that colonial English potters in the region had ever made such pieces, so it seemed that the only logical conclusion was that Native Americans were the producers of these pieces. These vessels and their fragments looked similar to the local Indian pottery. Ivor Noël Hume, the chief archaeologist at Colonial Williamsburg and the person tasked with interpreting it, decided to call this pottery "Colono-Indian Ware," and the name stuck. The dates that archaeologists assigned to the ware extended from the late seventeenth throughout the early nineteenth centuries, dates that conformed to the time of Indian–European contact and interaction.

Noël Hume's interpretation seemed to make sense, but he had a problem: archaeologists seldom found this pottery at Native American sites. Instead, they usually found it in areas associated with enslaved Africans. So the question became, How did enslaved individuals obtain this pottery? Noël Hume reasoned that Native American potters had produced it for sale and that African American community members had obtained it through trade. The consumers of this unique pottery therefore were thousands of individuals held against their will on the region's plantations. This interpretation, presented by one of the world's most renowned historical archaeologists, spurred a number of archaeologists to begin the search for the responsible Native American potters, and archaeologists identified one or two cultures in the American South who may have been the ware's creators.

By the early 1970s, however, some archaeologists had begun to rethink the cultural affiliation of Colono-Indian Ware. Well aware of the societal changes that had occurred, archaeologist Leland Ferguson proposed a new interpretation of the coarse, unglazed pottery called "Colono-Indian Ware." He proposed that enslaved Africans were not its *consumers* but rather its *producers*. He suggested that the name of the pottery should be changed to "Colono Ware" (archaeologists now generally call it "colonoware").

This novel, competing claim set many archaeologists on the path to finding and analyzing colonoware from the standpoint of African history, and some archaeologists were able to trace similar designs and styles directly to cultures in Africa. The link to Native Americans was still present, but archaeologists generally agreed that African potters were responsible for the vast majority of the sherds and vessels found on archaeological sites.

With time and much more study, archaeologists slightly backed away from the either/or interpretation of colonoware. By the 1980s, many archaeologists began to promote a new interpretation. This time, they focused on cultural blending, now thinking that colonoware was a hybrid version of European, African, and American Indian traditions. The idea that this pottery was a "creolized" artifact better suited archaeologists' inability to discern its true producers (because both Native American and African potters could make low-fired pottery in European shapes). This interpretation also conformed to the realities of cultural life in the Americas, where different cultures adopted various traits from one another.

The story of colonoware is important because it demonstrates how an archaeologist's preconceptions can affect his or her artifact interpretations. In each phase of colonoware's life, archaeologists altered its meaning even though the sherds themselves remained the same. This is true of all artifacts' life histories; colonoware is simply a good illustration.

Even though perspectives change, the tenets of the SEARCH protocol retain their importance. Archaeologists attempt to present interpretations that have the highest degree of plausibility based on what they know at the time. Just like everyone else, archaeologists cannot be certain their ideas are correct. No one alive today can know history with absolute certainty no matter how much they may wish it or how much time they spend studying it. Of course, the more research done, the more likely the increase in plausibility, but archaeologists can never be 100 percent certain that they are correct. Shoddy research in archaeology is like shoddy research in any endeavor, whether it's interpreting the meaning of the Great Pyramid or building a bookshelf. Understanding the rules of structured archaeological thinking—archaeo-thinking—increases the likelihood that our interpretations come as close to past reality as is possible given what we know at the time.

Continue Reading

Archaeology

Barker, Philip. 1982. *Techniques of Archaeological Excavation*. 2nd ed. New York: Universe.

Flinders Petrie, William Matthew. 1883. *The Pyramids and Temples of Gizeh*. London: Field and Tuer.

Romer, John. 2007. *The Great Pyramid: Ancient Egypt Revisited*. Cambridge: Cambridge University Press.

Colonoware

Ferguson, Leland. 1992. *Uncommon Ground: Archaeology and Early African America, 1650–1800*. Washington, DC: Smithsonian Institution Press.

Noël Hume, Ivor. 1962. An Indian Ware of the Colonial Period. *Quarterly Bulletin of the Archaeological Society of Virginia* 17: 2–14.

Thinking

Feder, Kenneth L. 2013. Help! I'm Being Followed by Ancient Aliens! *Skeptical Inquirer* 37, no. 2: 54–55.

Mills, Elizabeth Shown. 2012. *Evidence Explained: Citing History Sources from Artifacts to Cyberspace.* 2nd ed. rev. Baltimore: Genealogical Publishing.

Schick, Theodore, Jr., and Lewis Vaughn. 1995. *How to Think about Weird Things: Critical Thinking for a New Age.* Mountain View, CA: Mayfield.

White, Michael. 1999. *Weird Science: An Expert Explains Ghosts, Voodoo, the UFO Conspiracy, and Other Paranormal Phenomena.* New York: Avon.

UFOs

Jha, Alok. 2011. US Military to Launch Fastest-Ever Plane. *The Guardian,* August 10.

McGaha, James, and Joe Nickell. 2011. "Exeter Incident" Solved! A Classic UFO Case, Forty-Five Years "Cold." *Skeptical Inquirer* 35, no. 6: 16–19.

Peterson, Joseph. 1917. Some Striking Illusions of Movement of a Single Light on Mountains. *American Journal of Psychology* 28: 476–85.

Von Däniken, Erich. 1970. *Chariots of the Gods? Unsolved Mysteries of the Past.* Translated by Michael Heron. New York: Bantam.

Those Pesky Facts   **3**
Understanding Historical Facts

WHILE YOU WERE READING THE PREVIOUS CHAPTER, it may
have occurred to you that the concept of facts was missing. I
never described anything as a fact, even though the interpretations about the Great Pyramid and UFOs contain countless facts. Three of
the most basic facts about the pyramid are easy to list:

- It is located in Egypt.
- It is ancient.
- It contains a number of chambers and shafts on the inside.

Regarding UFOs, we can list these facts:

- People see them both during the day and at night.
- They usually appear as bright or blinking lights.
- People often report seeing them near airports.

In Berger's example, we saw that highly trained scholars can make different interpretations while looking at the same material objects—a McDonald's
hamburger, a bag of fries, and a milkshake. In each case, the interpreters drew
on certain facts they perceived as relevant in the process of creating their interpretations. In the office building, some of the scholars looked primarily at
the symbolism printed on the bag and cup, whereas others looked at the food
itself. The important point is that every interpreter, even UFO spotters, are
engaged in a process known as "fact selection." Although seemingly simple,
facts require careful thought because they are so numerous. The abundance
of facts means that selectivity is required when using them.

Can Facts Be Selected?

The concept of fact selection is a peculiar thing. Some people feel uncomfortable just thinking about it. After all, how can objective scholars pick which facts they wish to use in their interpretations? Doesn't the SEARCH formula make such a thing strictly out of the question?

People might become skeptical about the study of archaeology and history once they discover the existence of fact selection. Once they learn about it, some people may agree with Henry Ford that "history is bunk." (He also said, "History is more or less bunk." I guess he quantified history's "bunkiness" depending on his mood!) Most people who know what Ford said do not know his reasons for disparaging the study of history: he knew that historians, year after year, write new histories on the same subjects but with different perspectives. The publication of different histories of the same events, say, of the Napoleonic Wars, made Ford skeptical to the point of dismissal. If he had known the story of the McDonald's products on the picnic table, he might have had a better understanding of how people can employ the same facts to construct different interpretations or how they select a different set of facts from the same objects. He would also have understood that there is nothing *inherently* dishonest about the process (although there certainly can be).

Archaeologists, historians, and others involved in historical analysis have more flexibility when it comes to facts than do biologists and chemists. Fact selection is one important characteristic that separates hard scientists from archaeologists. A chemist who chooses to accept that water boils at 150°F will have significantly more problems professionally than an archaeologist who argues that the Egyptians were not as crazy about their Sun God as other archaeologists think. The boiling point of water is an established physical fact that cannot be refuted, whereas the Egyptians' loyalty to their Sun God may be argued about based on the evidence at hand.

One thing that makes fact selection difficult to understand is that it seems to imply that every fact has the same status as every other fact—that one fact is as good as any other. This kind of reasoning, which Professor Stebbing calls "potted thinking," is just plain wrong. (In her quaint British way, she uses "potted" to mean lazy or convenient. In the United Kingdom, potted meat is meat that can be conveniently bought in a can at the grocery store rather than from a butcher.) The professional chemist must accept that water boils at 212°F, not at 150°F, because the boiling point of H_2O is incontestable. The situation gets considerably murkier for archaeologists because the social sciences are not based on reproducible experiments. The past cannot be re-created in any complete way.

The idea that analysts select facts raises a number of interesting questions, the most obvious being, What are facts? Going back to UFOs, should we accept these two facts as equal?

1. UFOs are alien spaceships.
2. UFOs are really just misrecognized airplanes and other flying vehicles built by Earthlings.

These two statements obviously have different validity, but are they facts? In truth, the only true facts we have about UFOs are the following:

1. Lights appear in the sky.
2. People see them.

People extrapolate their interpretations from these two basic facts. Could it be that UFO spotters left out some facts? Perhaps they failed to report that they heard sounds when they saw the lights or that they may have had too much to drink at the time of their sighting. Perhaps they were tired, had a bright streetlight in their eyes, or weren't wearing their glasses. The point is that however much they may believe in their observations, the UFO spotters were engaged in fact selection. Why? Because fact selection is inevitable—for UFOs as it is for archaeologists.

Fact selection is a serious matter, and it has a number of key elements relevant to archaeo-thinking. The failure to appreciate its necessity and reality can have significant implications for archaeological interpretation.

To understand what fact selection is all about, we need to go back in time again just as we did to discover Professor Stebbing in chapter 1. In 1926, American historian Carl Becker presented a paper at the annual meeting of the American Historical Association in Rochester, New York. Titled simply "What Are Historical Facts?," he directed his comments to his professional colleagues, but his lessons are equally relevant to archaeologists.

Becker started by explaining what most people think a historian does: "He works in the past, he explores the past in order to find out what men did and thought in the past. His business is to discover and set forth the 'facts' of history." (At the time, most historians were men, and their perspectives were androcentric.) Except for his dated language, Becker's description is just as apt for archaeologists as for historians.

Becker notes that the word "facts" is usually uncontroversial because people understand it to mean "what is true." Most people in the Western world are familiar with the need "to get the facts straight," and they know "that the facts are what really matter." (Many older Americans will recall an old detective show in which the cops wanted "just the facts, ma'am.") So Becker is correct: most people intuitively understand a fact to be what is true or, in the case of history, what *was* true. Thus, facts are simply the individual pieces of the past that collectively make up history.

But for Becker, there's much more to what constitutes facts. For him, historical facts have a special meaning that historians (and archaeo-thinkers) must appreciate. He therefore challenges his colleagues to ponder this question: when we think about it, what, after all, is a historical fact? To investigate this question, he poses two related questions: 1) where is the historical fact, and 2) when is the historical fact?

Becker starts with a statement that almost every historian would consider to be a historical fact: "In the year 49 BC, Caesar crossed the Rubicon" (figure 3.1). This fact is so well known that it has entered everyday speech. We say that someone has "crossed the Rubicon" when he or she has done something that cannot be taken back; he or she is stuck with the consequences of his or her actions.

Becker takes this fact and says that it's not as factual as it may appear. The fact is actually a half-truth because, although Caesar did indeed cross the Rubicon (which is a small river in northern Italy), he did not go alone: he took a Roman legion with him. Once we have the image of Caesar crossing the river at the head of a Roman army, a number of questions immediately arise:

- How many people went with him?
- How long did the crossing take?
- Did they walk over a bridge?
- Was Caesar riding a horse?
- Did they go in boats, and, if so, where did they get the boats?
- If they used boats, what did they look like, and who made them?
- Did they have to pay to use the boats?
- If they went across the river on foot, how deep was it?

These are only some questions we may wish to have answered, and you can probably think up many more with ease. For example, think about the crossing from an archaeological point of view. What questions might be posed then?

Studies show that moving the Roman army around was not such an easy matter. In her book on the Roman army, Pat Southern directly addresses the logistical obstacles that Roman generals faced as they attempted

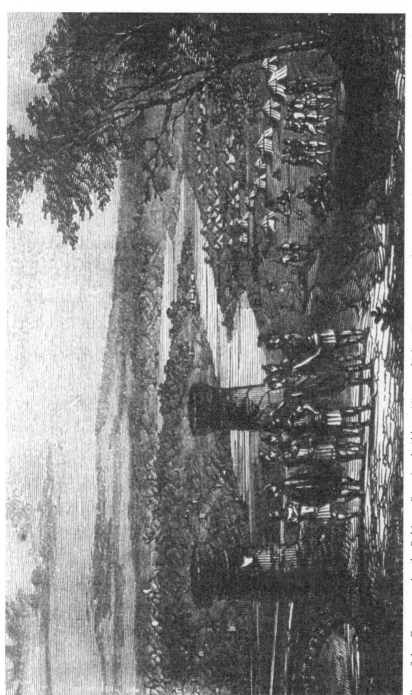

Figure 3.1.   Caesar crossing the Rubicon. From Jacob Abbott, *History of Julius Caesar* (New York: Harper and Brothers, 1869).

to move their armies from one place to another. She reports that some of what the Romans took with them were the following:

- Food
- Fodder for their animals
- Drink
- Tools for harvesting crops and hunting game
- Tools for processing and eating food
- Drinking and eating vessels
- Weapons
- Clothing
- Digging tools
- Medical and veterinary equipment
- One tent for each *contubernium* (a unit consisting of eight men)
- Field artillery for each century (100 men)
- A siege train with larger artillery if cities and citadels were to be stormed

This is only a partial list because each legionnaire undoubtedly carried a number of personal possessions. In any case, the list reveals that as Caesar and his men crossed the Rubicon, they undoubtedly took with them hundreds of artifacts, ranging from coins and cooking pots to pieces of artillery.

In addition to the artifacts themselves, archaeologists would be equally interested in the army's locations. If it took a number of days to move the entire legion across the river, at least two campsites—one on either side of the river—would have been necessary. Using the many techniques of site location available today, archaeologists should be able to locate the footprints of these "marching camps" to determine exactly where the crossing occurred. (The course of the river has changed since Caesar's time, so finding the exact spot of the crossing has been difficult.) But even once the campsites have been located, a systematic archaeological survey could identify the legion's route on each side of the river. Everything learned from the archaeological exploration would constitute historical facts. And, most excitingly, they would be entirely new facts. Only the Roman soldiers who made the crossing would have known the existence of what the archaeologists discovered.

Becker's question about Caesar and the Rubicon raises an important additional question: why did it matter that Caesar crossed the Rubicon? Surely, lots of people crossed it all the time, and some local residents may have crossed it several times each day. What makes Caesar's crossing so important that people around the world still use it as a catchphrase?

The implications of the crossing were immense. Becker explains that the Roman Senate had ordered Caesar to surrender his command of the Roman army in Gaul (the ancient province that is now France) because they did not want him outside their reach with a powerful army at his command. But Caesar refused to resign his command and instead made the fateful step of crossing the river (the Rubicon) separating the province of Gaul from imperial Rome. Crossing the Rubicon was thus an act of treason. But having made the fateful step, Caesar is thought to have said, "The die is cast," meaning that he had made a fateful decision from which he could not turn back. (As archaeo-thinkers, we might ask, on which side of the river did he say it, or did he say it during the crossing in the middle of the river?)

Crossing the Rubicon, then, is actually a *symbol* for thousands of related facts, some of which have tangible characteristics (artifacts, settlements, and campfires) and some of which do not (Caesar's words to his soldiers about their act of treason, the soldier's own comments, and so forth). As Becker shows, the historical fact about Caesar's crossing is not as simple as it first appears. It is a shorthand way of stating the thousands of related facts bundled into this one statement. The "big" fact revolves around the political implications of Caesar's crossing (which instituted an imperial era), but countless "smaller" facts are grafted onto the big one. Fact selection thus involves deciding which facts to use because all of them cannot be included. Too many facts exist.

Becker observes that historical facts are not as cold and hard as many scientific facts (e.g., the boiling point of water). The dimensions, temperatures, and weights of historical facts cannot be calculated despite their significance to our understanding of the past. This acknowledgment leads directly to Becker's second question: where is the historical fact?

In some ways, this is the most interesting question and the one that has captured the attention of many professional historians. Caesar's crossing of the Rubicon is known to have occurred on January 10, 49 BCE; it actually happened on that day. So where is this event now? Where does this fact exist?

At least two answers can be posited to answer this question. The first is to conclude that the event belongs entirely to the past, to the year 49 BCE. It is an event that actually occurred on that day in January. But where is that fact today? If we go to Italy, find the Rubicon, and, using advanced geophysical equipment, actually discover the precise spot at which Caesar and his legion crossed, will we see him crossing? Of course not. The crossing is part of history; it's gone forever. But the fact of the crossing remains.

So where is it? For Becker, the historical fact exists within someone's mind, "or it is nowhere, because when it is in no one's mind it lies in the records inert, incapable of making a difference in the world."

His last point is especially intriguing. If a historical fact actually happened, then it had been real. Historical events and practices were concrete occurrences, yet we cannot see, smell, or touch them. We can only imagine them.

We can begin to understand what Becker meant if we go back to archaeologist Walter Taylor's ideas mentioned in chapter 1. Taylor pointed out that the word "history" means different things. Becker's idea makes more sense if we recall two of these meanings. First, history is what really happened in the past. History is the sum total of the trillions of things that have actually occurred during the steady flow of time. Thus, the history that actually happened is "past actuality." If we think of human history in terms of past actuality, we can imagine the trillions of events that have occurred since the first *Homo sapiens* walked on two legs. The number of actions, ideas, and artifacts that make up past actuality is therefore truly mind-boggling.

To get an idea of just how mind-boggling, think about your day today. How many things did you do after you crawled out of bed? Think only about the act of brushing your teeth. How many events occurred as you did so, and how many objects were involved? Ten, 15, 20? Did you floss? Did you use mouthwash, and, if so, how many times did you swish it around in your mouth? What color is your toothbrush? How long is it? What brand is it? How many bristles does it have? And these questions concern only artifacts, not individual actions.

Each and every one of these things—no matter how insignificant they may seem—belong to past actuality because they really happened. They constitute part of human history in general and part of your own personal history specifically. They may not be important, and you may not remember them. No historian will ever write about them, but they occurred nevertheless.

A second meaning of history is "chronicle." To understand this meaning, how would you answer this question from a friend you met on the way to class: "What did you do last night?" How many facts should you relate? Would you recount in excruciating detail all the things that made up the past actuality of last night? Of course not. You would relate only certain things. These things, compiled together, constitute your chronicle—or story or narrative—of last night. In fact, it would be impossible for you to recount everything because, as anthropologist Alfred Kroeber once observed long ago, stating everything that "really happened"—every-thing—would take as long as the events themselves!

So when Becker says that historical facts reside in someone's mind, he's referring to the creation of chronicle, not to past actuality. If a historian chooses not to use a fact in his chronicle, just as you decided not to tell your friend everything about last night, it doesn't mean something didn't happen. You may have slipped and fallen in front of a crowded bar. This embarrassing event is part of past actuality but not part of your chronicle because you chose not to mention it in your "history" of last night. And because you did not select it, it lies inert in history; it is not likely to be used. Since the history of your fall was not written down anywhere (hope-fully it didn't end up on YouTube or Facebook), it recedes into the past and is forgotten (you hope). It will always have happened—you cannot change that—but it may never be part of a historical narrative.

Becker's views about fact selection are not simply interesting philo-sophical conundrums; they have real significance to archaeo-thinking. One of his most interesting ideas is that facts "lie inert" if not used. Archae-ologists can easily envision artifacts, hearths, storage pits, stone walls, and postholes lying inert in the soil until they are discovered during excava-tion. Each one of them is part of past actuality, but they are not part of a chronicle until they are unearthed and written about. They really do lie inert in the earth.

The difference between past actuality and chronicle was brought home to me, though I didn't realize it at the time, when I attended my very first archaeological excavation as a junior in college. The field director in charge of the project was interested in locating the remains of seventeenth-century houses inhabited by Native Americans at the time of the people's first encounter with French explorers. After eight weeks of excavation, the other students and I had uncovered a number of postholes and storage pits, many of which contained mixtures of European and Native American arti-facts. The field director was pleased with our results. I, on the other hand, thought we should have found more evidence. So I asked her, "what if we missed the best house by only a couple of inches?" Her reply was "Well, we don't know, do we?"

As I look back on this experience, I realize that I was experiencing the difference between past actuality and chronicle expressed archaeologi-cally. Viewed in material terms, all the postholes, storage pits, glass beads, animal remains, seeds, pollen, and everything else that remained at the site is part of past actuality. All these things are really there. The residents of the village had used them, and they were elements of past events that had actually taken place. But what we had collected from the site—the artifacts, the faunal and floral remains, the drawings, maps, and photographs—had become pieces of the site's chronicle. They became the evidence for past life at the village. This doesn't mean, of course, that the things we did not collect that summer are not part of the past because they most certainly are. It simply means they could not be part of the chronicle developed that summer because we did not have access to them. Being undiscovered, they were inert. Future archaeologists excavating the site would be able to add the newly found objects to their chronicle, and these additions would flesh out the overall historical and cultural picture of the village's past actuality. The chronicle compiled about the site will gain greater plausibility as the evidence piles up. With greater plausibility, archaeologists can have more confidence in their interpretations, even though everything about the past of that village can never be known.

Understanding the difference between chronicle and past actuality makes it possible to answer Becker's second question: "when is the historical fact?" The answer is "the present." Becker imagined that facts are "alive" today because they exist in the historian's head.

Viewed from the archaeologist's vantage point, Becker's question of "when" is especially interesting. Archaeologists are taught to think materially about people, things, and events, and when they hear the word "history," most immediately think about the material elements that compose it. When reading documents, historians tend to focus on what the document says and what it portrays about the writer and his or her times. Only in cases where they are attempting to determine whether a document is a forgery do they focus on its materiality—the type of paper, the formula of the ink, the design of the watermark, and so forth.

Archaeologists are equally concerned with what historical documents say and mean, but they are just as liable to think about the physicality of the books, letters, diaries, and all the other artifacts historians use. Historians usually focus on the ideas presented in documents rather than their material characteristics. The great historian-philosopher-archaeologist R. G. Collingwood perfectly expressed this perspective in his autobiography: "since history proper is the history of thought, there are no mere 'events' in history: what is miscalled an 'event' is really an action, and expresses some thought (intention, purpose) of its agent; the historian's business is therefore to identify this thought."

Archaeologists are also interested in past ideas, and many have spent their careers attempting to discover the ideas behind the creation, use, and deposition of material objects. The focus on materiality allows archaeologists to expand Becker's view that historical facts exist only in the present. After all, archaeologists have physical artifacts directly in front of them all the time, just as historians have documents before them in archives and libraries. Tangible pieces of history—potsherds, glass bottles, brass arrowheads, letters, diaries, and maps—exist in both the past and the present. The ability of artifacts to transcend time (to be inanimate time travelers) is a special characteristic of these historical facts. Unlike most historians, archaeologists spend a great deal of time measuring, describing, and comparing artifact types and publishing their results. Historians seldom do this. I've read hundreds of histories, and I've yet to find a single one that begins with a detailed, physical description of each document the historian has consulted. With some exceptions, most historians simply do not consider the material implications of the artifacts they use in their research. (After all, manuscripts are artifacts; they have been made by conscious human action.) This may seem like a minor point, and perhaps to some extent it is. But the material point of view is a key component of archaeo-thinking because all archaeological research—focused on whatever period of history and located wherever in the world—rests on the analysis and interpretation of physical things.

Is Fact Selection Dishonest?

Without knowing about Becker's perspective, just the mention of "fact selection" may imply something shady and unwarranted in a discipline like archaeology. Does this mean that archaeologists use only some evidence and ignore what doesn't fit their preconceived ideas? No legitimate researcher in any field should manufacture his or her facts to suit a research outcome or to substantiate a bizarre interpretation. Anyone who knowingly disregards findings that run counter to any claim—major or alternative—or who invents "evidence" should be immediately discredited as a poor researcher (at best) and an intellectual scoundrel (at worst).

Television programs and online videos about professional excavations reinforce the idea that archaeology is an exacting field of study, and in many important ways this is absolutely true. As noted above, archaeologists know that they destroy when they excavate. But the difference between past actuality and chronicle allows us to understand that perfectly reconstructing the past is impossible, even if we have amassed an incredible amount of information.

Returning to the world of fringe archaeology, it is clear that its proponents read into the evidence what they wish to see, ignoring the vast storehouse of archaeological evidence that has been collected over the past several decades. At Giza specifically, they ignore years of archaeological proof that 1) archaeologists have found artifacts related only to ancient Egyptian culture in the area; 2) absolutely no evidence suggests that the ancient Egyptians had nuclear capabilities, knowledge, or interest; and 3) no one, professional or otherwise, has ever found anything identifiable as "otherworldly" in Egypt or anywhere else. Pseudo-archaeologists have stepped out of the realm of past actuality and into the world of fantasy. They have composed chronicles filled with speculative half-truths, misrepresentations, and even nonsense. They have created their own facts, but these "facts" have come only from their imaginations, not from past actuality.

Contrary to the work of pseudo-archaeology, professional archaeologists must concern themselves with past actuality alone, understanding that it represents an immense universe of facts. Trillions of events, ideas, and actions make up past actuality, and to write history, one must extract certain things and downplay or disregard others.

Going back to Caesar and the Rubicon will help explain it. If you were an archaeologist of the Roman Empire and you were writing a book about the everyday dress of typical Roman legionnaires, you would be interested in what they wore during the crossing of the Rubicon rather than the route they took to get there. The route wouldn't cease to exist; rather, it would simply be unimportant *for your research*. But if you wanted to write about the soldiers' route, you would write about the specific places they stopped along the way. Their dress would have little significance to you. In any case, your selection is not dishonest in any way.

Archaeologists have always engaged in fact selection when they have described and classified artifacts. Description and classification are standard scientific procedures that necessarily include choosing some attributes and ignoring others. Selection is simply part of the archaeological process. An archaeological example is helpful.

Glass Beads and Glass Buttons

In 1970, Kenneth Kidd and Martha Kidd presented a classification of colonial-era glass trade beads. Their method was so good that archaeologists still refer to their work today, and like all classification systems, it rests on fact selection.

In the 1950s and 1960s, before historical archaeology had become the mainstream field it is today, archaeologists excavating early colonial sites often discovered tiny glass beads in great quantities, sometimes in the thousands.

They knew they had been made in Europe, shipped to North America, and traded to Native North Americans. Knowing the principles of seriation (see chapter 2), archaeologists understood that certain styles came into favor, were popular for a while, and then were replaced for something new. Beyond this, they knew very little. Unknown were how many styles of beads had been produced, the precise dates of their popularity, or the geographical spread of different beads. Were the beads found at an English trading post in upstate New York like those found at a Spanish mission site in Florida? To answer such questions, archaeologists required a standard way of describing the different bead styles. Only in this way could they make comparisons between sites.

The Kidds created a standard classification for use with colonial trade beads. Classifications, like seriations, require archaeologists to select certain characteristics as key attributes.

One of the attributes the Kidds selected as a distinguishing mark was whether a bead contained stripes (figure 3.2). Inspection of bead collections showed them that some beads have one stripe, whereas others have many stripes in various combinations of colors. For instance, Type Ib beads (tubular-shaped with stripes) have a number of different colored stripes: six black, three red, three white, three black, and so on. The Kidds paid close attention to the numbers and colors of stripes, but they did not select to measure the distance between the individual stripes. Their illustrations indicate that the distances vary (as logically they must given the different numbers of stripes), but they chose to ignore this fact in their classification. Stripe distance is a fact, so why did they ignore it? The answer is that they did not perceive "distance between stripes" as a significant variable. Were they wrong? No, they simply engaged in fact selection. Their failure to choose "distance between stripes" as a key attribute does not make the distance disappear. It is still there, lying dormant until another archaeologist decides to select this measure as an attribute of glass trade beads. The Kidds' failure to include stripe distance does not negate the value of their classification.

Another example comes from a much more common artifact, the simple glass button. Archaeologists for many years noticed a key attribute of this artifact but failed to appreciate its significance.

Archaeologists in the United States began excavating sites associated with enslaved Africans and African Americans in the late 1960s. By the mid-1980s, the archaeology of Africans in the New World had vastly expanded, and by 2000, archaeologists were excavating sites associated with people of African heritage throughout the United States, on the islands of the Caribbean, and across Central and South America. Archaeological

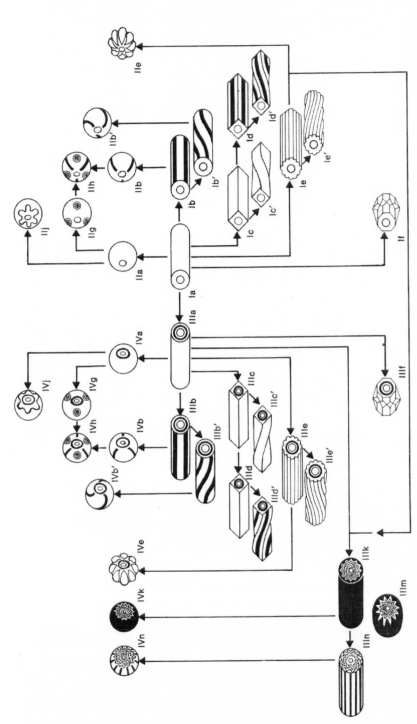

Figure 3.2. Part of Kidd and Kidd's glass bead classification system. Fig. 3. "Master Identification Chart for Tube Beads," p. 51. "A Classification System for Glass Beads for the Use of Field Archaeologists" by Kenneth E. Kidd and Martha Ann Kidd, *Canadian Historic Sites, Occasional Papers in Archaeology and History, No. 1,* pp. 45–89 (Ottawa: National Historic Sites Service, 1970). Used by permission, Parks Canada, Ottawa.

research has since provided abundant new information about the daily lives of Africans in the New World, including information about housing, food preparation, clothing, and diet. One of the questions archaeologists frequently asked during this research was, What features of African life were taken to the Americas? The search for such so-called Africanisms experienced several false starts and took many turns, but archaeologists were eventually able to appreciate how the study of belief systems might offer fresh information about African life outside Africa.

Since 1982, historical archaeologist Mark Leone has directed a highly successful program of excavation and interpretation in the colonial city of Annapolis, Maryland. He and his students have explored several sites associated with historically prominent people, but they have also spent a considerable amount of time and energy examining properties associated with people of African heritage. In the late 1990s, while excavating at the late eighteenth-century row house called the Slayton House, Leone and his students came on seven groups of artifacts. These objects, unremarkable by themselves, gained significance when found together. One group, found under the hearth of the house's kitchen, included a porcelain doll's head, arms, and legs (the cloth body had deteriorated); a ring; some pins; and a few glass buttons.

Archaeologists generally pay buttons little heed. Being common artifacts (just think how many a shirt has), they usually provide limited useful information. A button's type, whether it has a loop on its back or holes through it, can often reflect its date, and its size may reveal something about the type of garment to which it was attached. Archaeologists know that tailors sewed different-sized buttons on jackets, waistcoats, collars, coats, shirts, and knee breeches. The number of holes in a button is usually seen as merely a feature of manufacture, an attribute with little social, cultural, or historical value.

The archaeologist's dismissive attitude to the simple button changed, however, in the 1990s. Research on African American belief systems forced archaeologists to reconsider the meaning of the common four-holed button. In other words, archaeologists began to think about selecting button features as facts.

In the 1970s, folklife scholar John Vlach documented that people of African heritage often attributed magical powers to certain artifacts. A dime placed over someone's heart would protect against spells, beads worn around the neck would prevent sickness, and a brass ring worn on the left hand would forestall pains in the heart. Vlach also found information about buttons. White buttons, when worn around the neck, would bring luck and ease teething in children. Buttons with holes also could have special significance. For instance, the four holes in a common button form an X, or cosmogram. Many African cultures see this figure as representing the circle of life. The symbol, camouflaged as the holes in a button, could be secretly worn even on a plantation where the owner actively discouraged any expression of African heritage.

Some artifacts when grouped together could be especially powerful. Vlach noted that some people buried "spirit bundles" (also called "ritual caches"). These bundles, which contained common, everyday objects, were designed to protect people from harm. Certain artifacts were thought to provide protection from diseases (like smallpox), bad treatment (such as being whipped), or spells (like the evil eye).

Based on this information, Leone realized that various items he had found in his excavations were probably ritual caches rather than loose collections of objects that happened to be found together. At Annapolis, Leone found thousands of objects buried together under the kitchen and laundry of the Brice House. These deposits, dating from the 1880s to the 1920s, demonstrate the practice of protecting oneself with everyday objects. Since Vlach had made his observation about the importance of cosmograms, archaeologists have found examples under the floorboards of houses once inhabited by enslaved men and women. The increasing rate of archaeological discovery of ritual caches and cosmograms across the Western Hemisphere and in Africa itself indicates the widespread distribution of these important symbols.

The realization that some African peoples sought protection from the magical properties they perceived to lie in certain artifacts is an example of fact selection in action. What archaeologists once viewed as fairly insignificant pieces of past actuality—everyday objects like old four-holed buttons—have acquired significance as historical facts within the chronicle of African American life. Four-holed buttons now can be interpreted as part of a belief system. Before archaeologists understood this, they seldom if ever selected a button's holes as meaningful facts. The holes in a button were simply a fairly uninteresting feature of an extremely common artifact. Once they appreciated the holes' deeper meaning, archaeologists could select them as important historical and cultural facts.

We Really Do Select Facts?

So we see that fact selection is not the dishonest practice we may originally have thought. Although it would be naive to think that some researchers do not unfairly engage in politically or personally motivated fact selection (Holocaust deniers immediately come to mind), we must admit that fact selection is part of the normal research process, including for archaeologists. No one can ever know everything about the past, nor could they ever collect all possible pieces of past actuality. Some things are gone forever. Good archaeo-thinkers attempt to construct history from what they know at the time, with the understanding that their perspectives and interpretations are likely to be modified or completely changed as more information is collected. Fact selection is wrong only when it is done to present a false picture of the past. Fact selection is normal when archaeologists conduct it honestly with the intention of providing a deeper understanding of human history.

Continue Reading

Artifacts

Kidd, Kenneth E., and Martha Ann Kidd. 1970. A Classification System for Glass Beads for the Use of Field Archaeologists. *Canadian Historic Sites: Occasional Papers in Archaeology and History*, vol. 1, 45–89. Ottawa: National Historic Sites Service.

Leone, Mark P. 2005. *The Archaeology of Liberty in an American Capital: Excavations in Annapolis*. Berkeley: University of California Press.

Southern, Pat. 2007. *The Roman Army: A Social and Institutional History*. Oxford: Oxford University Press.

Vlach, John M. 1978. *The Afro-American Tradition in the Decorative Arts*. Cleveland, OH: Cleveland Museum of Art.

Fact Selection

Becker, Carl L. 1955. What Are Historical Facts? *Western Political Quarterly* 8: 327–40.

Collingwood, R. G. 1939. *An Autobiography*. Oxford: Oxford University Press.

Kroeber, A. L. 1935. History and Science in Anthropology. *American Anthropologist* 37: 539–69.

If p . . . Then What?   4
Archaeological Thinking and Logic

J UST AS IT IS TRUE FOR LIFE IN GENERAL, thinking logically is an integral part of the archaeological research process. Ivor Noël Hume, universally considered one of the founders of historical archaeology, once observed that "archaeology is really an incredibly simple use of logic, and if you don't have that, you don't do very well." He is absolutely correct.

Our Love of Logic
People living in Western cultures tend to admire logical thinkers. After all, the pedigree of logic extends all the way back to Aristotle, Plato, and many other philosophers who lectured in ancient Greece and Rome. Westerners generally believe that logical thinking is a trait worth acquiring. As early as 1662, Antoine Arnauld and Pierre Nicole, the authors of *The Port-Royal Logic*, referred to logic as "the art of thinking." Author Lewis Carroll (yes, the same guy who wrote *Alice in Wonderland*) described logical thinking as "mental recreation" and said that once you have mastered it, "you have a mental occupation always at hand, of absorbing interest, and one that will be of real *use* to you in *any* subject you may take up."

Clear thinking is important to archaeologists because their efforts to piece together the past from the often-fragmentary remains left behind requires inference as well as the ability to make connections between things, ideas, and actions. Regardless of their theoretical orientation, logical thinking helps archaeologists strengthen their arguments and to have more confidence in their interpretations. Because archaeologists can never go back and experience the past directly, their perceptions of history rest solely on the mental images they create about it. Their arguments therefore must be well conceived, properly structured, and clearly expressed.

Archaeologists use both deductive and inductive logic, though they rely most strongly on inductive reasoning. The goal of this chapter is to introduce you to the role of logic in archaeo-thinking but not to make you into a logician. Archaeologists do not wish to become logicians, and many of the logicians' philosophical concerns are far beyond what archaeologists need to know. Nevertheless, understanding some of the basic rules of logical thinking is an important step toward developing your skills as an archaeo-thinker. These skills will help you "to think to some purpose."

Deducing

The first thing to appreciate about deductive logic is that it deals with the structure of arguments rather than with the truth of their conclusions. Logic offers the tools for assessing the relation between statements of evidence (termed "premises") and conclusions. The term "argument" specifically refers to a series of premises that have an attached conclusion, not to a verbal dispute.

A deductive argument is "valid" when it has the correct form and "invalid" when its form is incorrect. Deduction does not involve what is "true" or "false." Deduction concerns itself only with form, not with truth. Even so, the correct logical form of a deductive argument can guide and structure an archaeologist's thinking.

The goal of deductive argumentation is to establish true conclusions based on true premises. False premises are simply that: false. The implications of false premises in the world of pseudo-archaeology can be easily seen because its proponents present wildly speculative claims about space aliens, vanished mysterious civilizations, and other implausible interpretations of the past. They use speculation for their premises, develop arguments that defy archaeological reality, and create false pictures of the past. Today's professional archaeologists understand the pitfalls of wild speculation (see chapter 1) and avoid them by understanding logical argumentation.

In deductive reasoning, the conclusion must be true if the premises are true. A deductive argument can have a true conclusion but be invalid, just as it can have a false conclusion and be valid (as a logical argument form). A valid deductive argument cannot have true premises and a false conclusion, but it can have false premises and a true conclusion. To make sense of this, consider the following three arguments:

(1) All artifacts are made or modified by humans [true]
    All arrowheads are artifacts [true]
    Therefore, all arrowheads are made or modified by humans [true]
(2) All arrowheads are glass [false]
    All windows are arrowheads [false]
    Therefore, all windows are glass [true]
(3) All arrowheads are brass [false]
    All artifacts are arrowheads [false]
    Therefore, all artifacts are brass [false]

Each of these arguments is logically valid because of its structure. Validity is determined by the form, not by what the argument says, for clearly all windows are not arrowheads. Given the nature of deduction, however, if the premises are true, then the conclusion must be true. A valid deductive argument cannot have true premises and a false conclusion.

Archaeologists seldom have the luxury of being able to use the logical form "All . . . are," but the above examples demonstrate how deduction works. Archaeologists, faced with the huge number of facts present in past actuality, can almost never assert 100 percent certainty except about the most mundane things. Archaeologists can be certain only when speaking about a finite collection of objects, such as a collection of 200 arrowheads, but not when it comes to situations where they cannot assert that they know absolutely everything about a site (which is an impossibility).

Much more important to archaeologists are "if/then" arguments, termed "conditional statements." Conditional statements are used in "conditional arguments," and conditional arguments have valid and invalid forms. In an interpretive field like archaeology, the structure of the argument can affect its inherent sense.

The most basic form of a conditional argument is the following:

If p, then q [the conditional statement]
p
$\therefore$ [Therefore] q

In this argument, p is called the "antecedent" and q the "consequent." The above form is a valid form called "affirming the antecedent." An archaeological example is the following:

If arrowheads are made of brass [p], then they are metallic [q]
These arrowheads are made of brass [p]
Therefore, they are metallic [q]

In this argument, we have affirmed the first part of the conditional statement, the antecedent. A second valid argument is called "denying the
consequent." This argument has the following form:

If p, then q
Not q
∴ Not p

An archaeological example is the following:

If arrowheads are made of brass [p], then they are metallic [q]
These arrowheads are not metallic [not q]
Therefore, they are not made of brass [not p]

The two invalid forms of these deductive arguments are called "the fallacy
of affirming the consequent" and "the fallacy of denying the antecedent."
The first form is the following:

If p, then q
q
∴ p

In archaeology,

If arrowheads are made of brass [p], then they are metallic [q]
These arrowheads are metallic [q]
Therefore, they are made of brass [p]

This is faulty deductive reasoning because the arrowheads can be metallic,
but they might be bronze or iron; they do not have to be brass. The second
invalid form is the following:

If p, then q
Not p
Not q
If arrowheads are made of brass [p], then they are metallic [q]
These arrowheads are not brass [not p]
Therefore, they are not metallic [not q]

As is true of the first example, the arrowheads could be a different metal
than brass and still be metallic.

You see in the two valid arguments that true premises lead to true conclusions, but in the two invalid forms, a false premise leads to a false conclusion.
Invalid arguments provide false conclusions because some metallic artifacts

can be made of iron, copper, or some other metal. But remember, the goal of deduction is to create valid arguments, not necessarily to derive the truth. We can examine the if/then argument form further by illustrating a popular invalid argument from the world of pseudo-archaeology. It has become common for ancient astronaut theorists to argue that people who had the ability to fly must have built all the massive ancient monuments that are best seen from the air. They say that because Earthlings did not have the ability to see the Earth from the sky before 1782—when the Montgolfier brothers flew the first hot-air balloon—native peoples could not have been responsible for building the monuments. Their argument takes this form:

If large monuments are best seen in their entirety from the air [*p*], then they must have been constructed by a culture that had the ability of flight [*q*]
The biggest ancient monuments are best seen from the air [*q*]
Therefore, big monuments must have been built by a culture with the ability of flight [*p*]

This looks like a perfectly valid deductive argument because it affirms the antecedent. The problem, of course, is that the antecedent is based on pure speculation. Remember that if the premises are true, then the conclusion must also be true. But in this example—and indeed in all pseudo-archaeology—the premises are merely speculative. They derive from imagination, not past actuality.

Pseudo-archaeologists have made this claim about many ancient sites, including the world-famous Serpent Mound in southern Ohio (figure 4.1). This mound is a long earthwork resembling a curly snake holding something that looks like an egg in its mouth. Archaeologists date the mound to about 1000 CE and associate it with the Adena Culture. Ancient astronaut theorists argue that space aliens must have built the mound because the best view of it is from the air. (They say this despite the fact that Squier and Davis, mentioned in chapter 1, made a scale drawing—as if seen from the air—almost 40 years before the flight of the first hot-air balloon!) Since the conclusion of a valid deductive argument must be true if the premises are true, it becomes impossible to create a valid argument with only the pseudo-archaeologist's premises. To affirm the antecedent, it would have to be true that space aliens built the mound:

If space aliens built the Serpent Mound [*p*], then you could see its full 1/4-mile extent best from the sky [*q*]
Space aliens built the Mound [*p*]
Therefore, you can see its full extent best from the air [*q*]

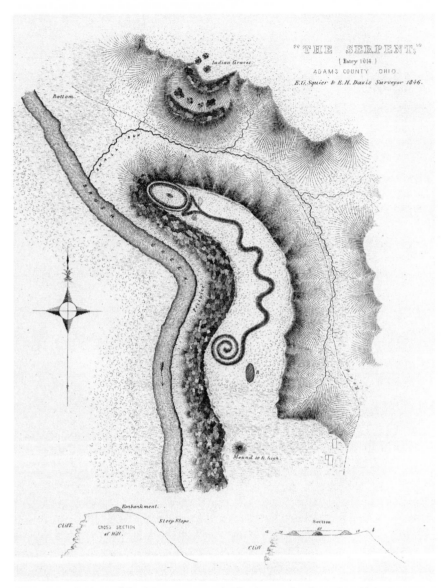

Figure 4.1.   Squier and Davis's 1846 map of "The Serpent," Adams Co., Ohio. In *Ancient Monuments of the Mississippi Valley: Comprising the Results of Extensive Original Surveys and Explorations* by Ephraim G. Squier and Edwin H. Davis, Smithsonian Contributions to Knowledge, vol. 1 (Washington, DC: Smithsonian Institution, 1848), facing p. 96.

Professional archaeologists cannot accept that ancient aliens built anything on Earth because no one anywhere has ever found any credible evidence for these space creatures.

In a classic study in American archaeology, James Deetz investigated the changing relationships between two variables—postmarriage residence (where newlyweds live after marriage) and pottery design—among the eighteenth-century Arikaras of the Great Plains. This was the era the Arikaras were first encountering Europeans.

Deetz's claim about Arikara culture was that greater diversity in pottery design should be explainable by a transition from matrilocality (living with the wife's family or village) to a less structured form of postmarriage settlement. The Arikaras underwent social reorganization after European contact because the introduction of smallpox had caused massive depopulation. Villages losing members tended to unite with others suffering a similar fate. Deetz's inference was that young girls in matrilocal settings learned pottery designs from their mothers and grandmothers, but in the absence of matrilocality (because of depopulation and village dispersal), the girls learned pottery design from women from a number of different villages (and thus from unrelated kin groups). He reasoned that the increase in the number of design sources (contributed by woman potters from different villages) should occur as matrilocality broke down.

Deetz posited that the change in Arikara culture should be reflected in their pottery as an increase in the number of pottery designs. In other words, if the pottery sample excavated from a site dating before European contact had 10 design motifs and a second site dating after European contact and depopulation had 23 motifs, then his supposition about the relationship between cultural change and pottery design would have some merit. Deetz's central claim is a conditional argument:

If residence location by women after marriage changed, then pottery decorations should have been affected.

The only way Deetz can resolve the argument is with the fallacy of affirming the consequent:

If postmarriage residence changes [*p*], then pottery design will become more diverse [*q*]
Pottery design becomes more diverse [*q*]
Therefore, the Arikaras experienced a change in their post-marriage residence rules [*p*]

He must make this mistake because the collection and examination of pottery sherds will determine whether their designs actually became more diverse through time. To make his argument a valid form, he would have to start with the pottery design and work toward a change in postmarriage residence.

In truth, archaeologists seldom use pure deductive logic. The example taken from Deetz's research was not truly a deductive exercise because much of his information relied on induction. Nevertheless, his argument demonstrates the care archaeologists must take when they say they are working deductively. The use of "if . . . then" statements must be used with extreme caution in serious archaeological thinking.

Not Deduction, the Other One . . .

Deductive reasoning is extremely difficult for archaeologists to use because the premises must include the same information as the conclusions. The failure of archaeologists to know everything about the past (to have 100 percent confidence) shows why archaeologists rely mostly on inductive reasoning.

Inductive arguments are much more useful to archaeologists because the information they contain in their conclusions may exceed the information in the premises. Examples of inductive arguments appear in every article or book written about archaeological research. As with deduction, however, archaeologists must avoid certain pitfalls.

You will recall that in a deductive argument, if the premises are true, then the conclusion must also be true. For space aliens to have built the Great Pyramid, it must be true that 1) they exist, 2) they came to Earth with the expressed purpose of building gigantic monuments in the Egyptian desert, and 3) they left behind no other traces of their extremely advanced culture. Each of these premises is false. In an inductive argument, true premises may or may not lead to a true conclusion.

A correct inductive argument will add confidence or support to a true conclusion; it should lead to a conclusion that is probably true, but in induction, true premises can lead to a false conclusion. In archaeology, this means that an excavator's premises may be true even though he or she has drawn a false conclusion from it.

The simplest form of inductive argument in archaeology is "induction by enumeration." This is simply where a researcher infers a conclusion about all the members of a class from the observed members. For example, an archaeologist might report that "80 percent of ceramic sherds excavated at the Harris Site are pearlware" (a white-bodied ceramic popular in the nineteenth century) and use induction by enumeration to infer that 80 percent of all possible sherds at the site (those that have been collected and those that have yet to be excavated) are pearlware. This argument takes this form:

80 percent of the ceramics excavated from the Harris Site are pearlware.

Therefore, 80 percent of all ceramics at the Harris Site (including those that remain unexcavated, or "inert" as Becker would say) are pearlware.

Archaeologists make this kind of argument all the time. They conduct walkover surveys and small test excavations in an effort to extrapolate from the collected sample to the entire site. However, the nature of archaeological research—and the very nature of induction by enumeration itself—means that true premises can lead to a false conclusion. At the Harris Site, the archaeologist may simply have excavated in the area that contained most of the pearlware at the site, perhaps a trash dump filled when the site's residents threw out their old dishes and replaced them with the newest, most fashionable whiteware (see chapter 7). Given this possibility, archaeologists understand that the larger the sample size, the greater confidence they can have in their inferences. An archaeologist can usually have greater confidence in a 50 percent sample than in a 5 percent sample.

Induction by enumeration is not without problem because statistics can be manipulated. Mark Twain famously said, "There are three kinds of lies: lies, damned lies, and statistics." (He erroneously attributed this quote to British Prime Minister Benjamin Disraeli, but no one knows who first said it. Regardless, the sentiment is clear!)

The most serious problem with enumeration is the "fallacy of insufficient statistics." This means drawing a conclusion from scanty evidence. An archaeologist with only a 1 percent sample would be foolish to make sweeping claims based on such a small amount of evidence. Broad claims with weak evidence are likely to lead to suspect conclusions. Consider these two examples:

(1) 5 percent of the ceramic sherds from the Harris Site are pearlware. Therefore, all of the ceramics that exist at the Harris Site are pearlware.

(2) 5 percent of the potsherds from the Harris Site are pearlware. Therefore, all Scottish settlers in the United States used pearlware.

The second conclusion is clearly the shakiest of the two, though both are based on the flimsy evidence of insufficient statistics. Still, both conclusions may be correct even if the premises are incorrect.

For many years, archaeologists have wrestled with the question "how much is enough?" when deciding whether to have confidence in the results of a survey or excavation. An archaeologist who draws conclusions from an 85 percent sample usually can have more confidence than someone who extrapolates from a 5 percent sample. Archaeologists are often forced into making claims based on limited evidence because of shortages in time, funds, and resources. It is important to realize, though, that even large samples can be biased and that small samples can provide important information. Unfortunately, no magic number exists to indicate the "proper" sample size. Each situation is unique, and archaeologists must make careful decisions about how definite to be in their interpretations.

Two inductive argument forms are more prevalent in archaeology than enumeration. They are also more problematic. The difficulties arise from assessing whether the conclusions reached are justified or based on personal bias.

The first argument is called the "argument from authority." This argument form is straightforward:

X says p
$\therefore p$

Converting this to English, we might say the following:

Dr. Miller says I have an ear infection,
Therefore, I have an ear infection.

Archaeologists (and all scholars) implicitly use this argument form every time they cite someone else's research. To do so, they make the assumption that the cited person is a legitimate authority on the subject being discussed. In the above case, we accept that Dr. Miller has a medical degree from an accredited institution, holds a current and legitimate license to practice, and knows an ear infection when she sees one.

Archaeologists regularly make the same assertions in their research. In fact, relying on the works of prior authorities is an important characteristic of all scientific and scholarly research. For example, in a publication of mine, I wrote,

> *Maritime archaeologists are conducting serious and important research around the globe and diligently working to convince the public that maritime archaeological sites are as important to the world's cultural heritage as land-based remains* (e.g., Adams 2002; Corbin and Rodgers 2008; Flatman and Staniforth 2006; McConkey and McErlean 2007; Richards 2008; Staniforth 2003; Staniforth and Nash 2006; Van Tilburg 2007; Webster 2008; Williams 2007).

In this statement, I regard all the cited men and women as authorities on maritime archaeology. I assume that each of them has extensive knowledge of and experience in the field, so I feel completely comfortable mentioning their names and publications to support my assessment about maritime archaeology. Since this is not my area of expertise, I am willing to rely on the authority of others.

In truth, an argument from authority has a premise that actually comes before the premise "*X* says *p*." This initial premise is something like "*X* is a recognized, reliable authority on subject *p*." This means that the prestige of *X* (in my case, Adams and the other archaeologists I cited) is secure enough in the field of *p* (maritime archaeology) to be referenced as an authoritative scholar on maritime archaeology.

Arguments by authority, however, have an inherent problem: how do we know that someone is an authority on something? Should we accept *X* as an authority on *p*?

Celebrity product endorsements are easy places to see the problem. The reputation of famous actors, sports figures, and politicians often transfers beyond their areas of expertise. For example, the basketball great Michael Jordan is famous for his promotion of a certain brand of men's underwear. Advertisers are clever enough to know that most people recognize his name and that they are therefore likely to associate him with something special. Advertising executives thus exploit the transfer of prestige from basketball to underwear. But if we stop and think about it, we must ask ourselves, Is Michael Jordan really a reliable authority on the subject of underwear? To put this question in the form of a comparison, Should we have greater confidence in someone who works in the underwear industry but is unknown to the world at large or in Michael Jordan, who, though unique in the world of basketball, is just like millions of other men who wear underwear?

We can return to the world of speculative archaeology to explore the problem further. Consider these three authors and their famous books: Erich von Däniken, who jump-started the current fascination with alien astronauts with *Chariots of the Gods?*; Barry Fell, who, in *America B.C.*, argued that ancient Celts and other Old World peoples visited North America thousands of years before Columbus; and Gavin Menzies, who developed an entirely new line of speculative inquiry with *1421: The Year China Discovered America*. Each of these authors is a talented and engaging writer, and their books, though frustrating for professional archaeologists, can be fun to read as pure speculation. Should we conclude, however, that each man is an authority on archaeology and ancient history? One way to answer this question is to examine their archaeological training. Before finding fame as writers, none of these men had any experience as archaeologists. Von Däniken was a hotel manager, Fell was a professor of invertebrate zoology at Harvard University, and Menzies was a lieutenant commander in Her Majesty's Royal Navy. If I wanted advice about a hotel, information on fossil sea urchins, or to learn about daily life onboard a submarine, I would judge each of these men as expert authorities. I could assume that each man knew more than me about each subject.

Unwary readers might be led to conclude that Fell is a reliable authority because he was a Harvard professor or that Menzies's military credentials add credibility to his interpretations. The key point to remember, however, is that both men are dabbling in realms outside their areas of expertise. They write about archaeological subjects but without the professional's background or experience. The general public is misled by the writers' speculations. But each man's interpretation of human history is seriously flawed (by professional standards) and illogical (by nature). Neither Menzies, Fell, nor von Däniken can be considered a legitimate archaeological authority regardless of how much each has written or how believable readers may deem their accounts. Their economic success cannot diminish or erase the fallacies in their interpretations.

Determining who is an authority can be difficult because someone may be formally untrained in a subject but still knowledgeable about it. Unlike civil engineering or accounting, archaeologists are not required to pass certification tests. Myriad television programs and Internet videos demonstrate that almost anyone can claim to be an archaeologist without any training at all.

The difficulty in determining expertise is made even more complex because professional archaeologists often rely on nonprofessionals for information. Local residents know a great deal about their regions and their histories and traditions. Amateur archaeologists or avocationalists can be extremely knowledgeable yet professionally untrained; they can be self-taught experts. A powerful but unique example comes from the personal history of Ivor Noël Hume, mentioned at the beginning of this chapter as an archaeological pioneer and a world-renowned authority. He started his professional life as a stage manager for a London theater, not as an archaeologist. He began in archaeology as an untrained volunteer while waiting for his big break on the stage. His opportunity never came, and luckily for archaeology, he fell into a job with the London Museum. He now has decades of experience, a number of prominent books, and a host of awards to his credit. Despite his background, no one in his or her right mind would consider him anything but a true authority on historical archaeology and British ceramics. He learned through dedication, self-education, and on the job.

Given the difficulties, how do we decide who is an authority on a particular subject and who is a pretender? In his book *Logic*, Wesley Salmon offers clues to assess whether someone is an authority. Putting these clues in the form of questions helps to clarify them:

1. Is the person making a statement so famous they experience a "transfer of prestige"? (Does Michael Jordan's fame as a basketball great translate into knowledge about underwear? In other words, is his fame in one area simply migrating to another area? Has he actually spent time in the underwear industry learning its ins and outs?)
2. Is the person making a statement about something speaking outside his or her area of expertise? (Should Barry Fell have stuck with his sea urchin research and left ancient history to scholars better trained in the subject?)
3. Has the person received enough training outside his or her area of expertise to make them an expert on something? Should we accept their expertise in the absence of formal education? (Ivor Noël Hume has proved his expertise despite not having an advanced degree in archaeology.)
4. Is the person making a statement about something for which they could not possibly have any information? (How can Erich von Däniken know that space aliens exist when no one else has been able to prove it and no physical evidence exists?)

Answers to these questions will clarify whether we can justifiably consider someone an expert in a particular subject. Unfortunately, the resolution of the questions may never be wholly satisfactory. Most readers are willing to accept the word of authors who write authoritatively and seem credible. For example, Menzies's expertise as a naval officer suggests that he knows a great deal about ocean currents, and he probably does have this knowledge. But the key question is, Should we allow his knowledge of the ocean to transfer over into ancient history and archaeology? Is his knowledge great enough for us to accept that Ming dynasty Chinese sailors visited North America 70 years before Columbus?

An additional difficulty with assessing whether an argument from authority is legitimate stems from the problem that true authorities can disagree. Archaeologists, like all scholars, are perfectly free to change their opinions as they acquire more information and rethink things. Because archaeologists can never know the past with certainty, they must often hedge their bets and make inferences based on sample size, their knowledge of the works of others, and their own research.

Sincere differences of opinion by committed, knowledgeable scholars create dissenting camps that can cause hard feelings lasting for years. The processual archaeology of the late 1960s (see chapter 1) created two opposing camps—"new-style" processual archaeologists and "old-style" culture historians—just as during the same era the development of historical archaeology created an equally tense relationship between anthropological archaeologists and archaeological historians. The disputes between these groups were often ill-tempered, as each struggled to demonstrate they were right and the other side was misguided at best and terribly wrong at worst. As Wesley Salmon points out, what often happens in these situations is the development of an "argument by consensus." As dissenting camps form, the entire group, rather than a lone individual, is regarded as an authority. This approach, however, also has problems. It can take years for a single individual going against the consensus (but ultimately correct in his or her interpretation) to get his or her views accepted by most authorities within a specific field.

Some archaeologists argued for years that the only way the first inhabitants of North America could have arrived in the continent was by crossing the Bering land bridge and traveling through an ice-free corridor in the middle of the Alaskan peninsula. In the 1960s, a few archaeologists began to question this "mid-continental hypothesis," instead suggesting a coastal route. In 1979, writing in *American Antiquity*, American archaeology's premier journal, archaeologist Knut Fladmark made a strong case for considering an entryway along the Pacific coast. His interpretation failed to take hold as the consensus view. Brian Fagan, the best-selling archaeologist-author, did not even mention the idea in his *The Great Journey: The Peopling of Ancient America* (published in 1987). But the idea of a coastal migration route never died out, and research conducted by a team of archaeologists and geologists showed in 2012 that ecological conditions would have made a coastal migration route entirely possible. As a result of this and other findings, archaeologists are now less inclined to dismiss the coastal route outright, but even reaching this point has taken over 40 years of analysis, argumentation, and reinterpretation. That Fagan mentioned the coastal route in his *The First North Americans* (published in 2011) demonstrates that mainstream attitudes have indeed changed. (Recent DNA evidence adds further weight to the idea that at least some people came across the Bering land bridge. The controversy about other routes rages on, however.)

The nature of archaeological research, like all scholarly endeavors, mandates that change in interpretation can occur slowly. It may take years to establish one's credentials as an authority in a particular field, and, once accomplished, it may take even more time for a new interpretation to become the consensus view. This process, however, characterizes how knowledge grows over time.

The creation of intellectual camps around a particular subject, such as the introduction of humans into North America, can lead to a kind of inductive argument called "the argument against the person" (older books list it as "the argument against the man"). This argument takes the following form:

X says p
$\therefore$ not p

This argument maintains that whatever X says about p should be disregarded because X is known to be consistently wrong in his or her interpretations. This argument is a difficult one to sustain except in the most extreme circumstances. For instance, someone who insists that the sun will rise in the west tomorrow morning cannot be trusted as an authority on astronomy. Being consistently wrong about the sun, day after day, has created a lack of confidence in that person's judgment.

The argument against the person must relate specifically to the matter at hand. It would be unwise to reject something someone says simply because we do not like his or her political affiliation, religious beliefs, or organizational memberships. People may do this all the time, but it is logically unwise. Individuals may wish to discount what a politician says about nuclear safety simply because his or her position on gun control is unpopular. We humans have the right to think illogically when it comes to the mundane circumstances of daily life, but a lack of logic in archaeology carries the consequence of affecting how the history of the world and our place within it is perceived and understood.

Salmon points out the difficulty of labeling someone an "anti-authority." Affixing the label can be tricky because no one can ever be 100 percent certain the person has *always* been wrong. Salmon observes, though, that scientific cranks are one instance where the label can be applied without undue danger. Cranks

1. usually reject all established science or some area of it;
2. tend to be ignorant of the science they reject, generally believing that it's just wrong on a gut level but not being able to provide concrete details;
3. have no access to recognized publication outlets for scientific research and are not invited to scholarly meetings;

4. think the opposition they receive from the professional scientific community is based on the bias and closed-mindedness of scholars; and
5. oppose science because of a belief or beliefs based on religious or political views.

To Salmon's five characteristics, we can add a sixth one specific to archaeology:

6. belief that archaeologists are engaged in a conspiracy to cover up the true history of humanity.

It's easy to find evidence of Salmon's claims in the books of pseudo-archaeologists. For instance, Von Däniken writes in *Chariots of the Gods?*, "It took courage to write this book. . . . Because its theories and proofs do not fit into the mosaic of traditional archaeology, constructed so laboriously and firmly cemented down, scholars will call it nonsense and put it on the Index of those books which are better left unmentioned." In their book *Forbidden Archaeology: The Hidden History of the Human Race*, authors Michael Cremo and Richard Thompson complain about a widespread archaeological conspiracy to keep their interpretations out of the scholarly press. Whether such writers are true cranks or simply misguided history buffs is a judgment call, but true cranks are known in the history of archaeology.

One of the most famous cranks in American history—and one with a connection to archaeology—was a man named Ignatius Donnelly. Donnelly, who was born in 1831 and died in 1901, initially gained fame as a politician, having run for and won several state and federal offices. A friend to Abraham Lincoln, Donnelly served as lieutenant governor of Minnesota and a member of the U.S. Congress. His real claim to fame—and the reason he is today widely regarded as the Prince of Cranks—was his speculative writings, especially *Atlantis: The Antediluvian World*, published in 1882 (figure 4.2). Just about everything people believe today about Atlantis comes from Donnelly's imagination rather than from Plato, the only original source on the lost civilization. *Atlantis* was a major best seller when it first appeared and the book is still available today.

In keeping with the spirit of the late nineteenth century, Donnelly embraced science with gusto, realizing he could use the public's optimistic belief in it to exploit their gullibility. Today's cranks have learned from Donnelly to be more sophisticated, and rather than openly accepting science as Donnelly chose to do, they have decided to tap into an undercurrent of suspicion about science and intellectual scholarship. Like Donnelly, though, they still use science selectively, letting their imaginations do most of the work.

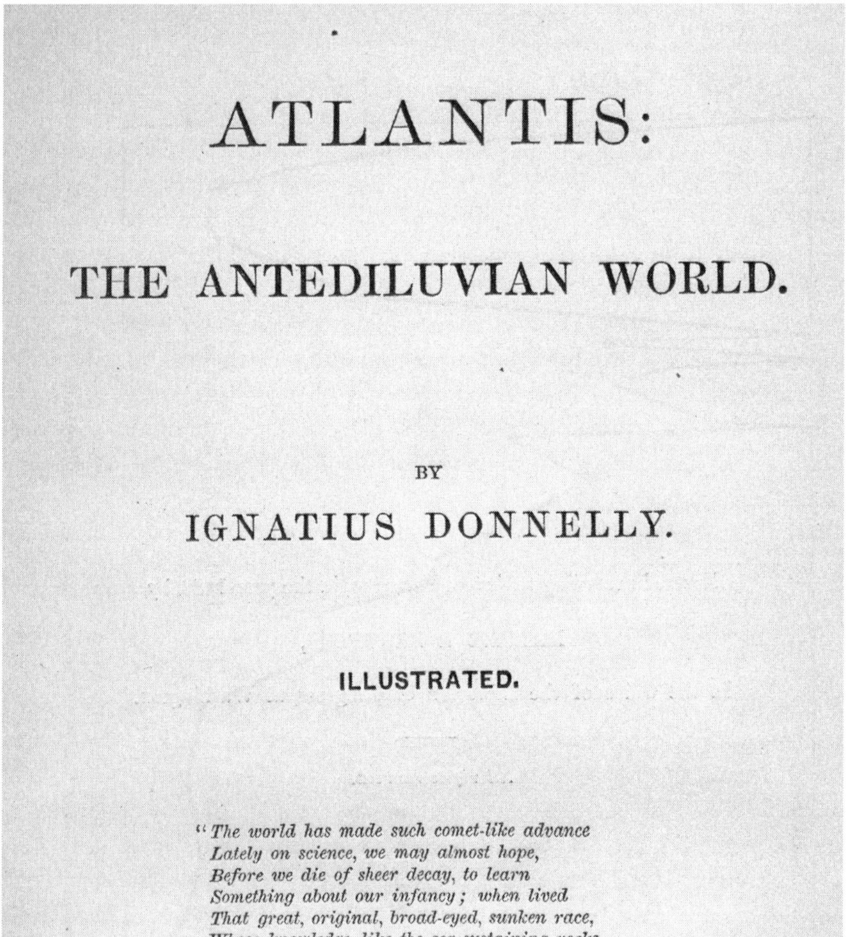

ATLANTIS:

THE ANTEDILUVIAN WORLD.

BY

IGNATIUS DONNELLY.

ILLUSTRATED.

" The world has made such comet-like advance
Lately on science, we may almost hope,
Before we die of sheer decay, to learn
Something about our infancy ; when lived
That great, original, broad-eyed, sunken race,
Whose knowledge, like the sea-sustaining rocks,
Hath formed the base of this world's fluctuous lore."
FESTUS.

NEW YORK:

HARPER & BROTHERS, FRANKLIN SQUARE.

1882.

Figure 4.2. Title page of Ignatius Donnelly's *Atlantis: The Antediluvian World* (New York: Harper and Brothers, 1882).

I've Been Abducted

Before leaving logic behind, another set of concepts in worth mentioning. In the late nineteenth century, an American philosopher named Charles S. Peirce explained what he called "abduction." Rather than having anything to do with space aliens, Peirce identified abduction as a kind of reasoning. His views, though controversial among philosophers, have relevance to archaeological thinking.

Peirce understood that not every claim that can be dreamed up is equally suitable to providing reasonable interpretations. Proposing that not all claims are created equal, he concluded that propositions that are more "economical" than the others are most likely the best ones. In his sense, "economical" means the simplicity and conservatism of the SEARCH formula presented in chapter 2.

Philosopher Cameron Shelley has directly applied abductive reasoning to archaeology by exploring "visual abduction." This form of inference is common in archaeological research.

Archaeologists use mental frameworks and pattern recognition to identify specific classes of objects. Field surveying is the easiest place to see visual abduction in progress. When archaeologists walk a field looking for artifact scatters and other evidence of past settlements, they do not know precisely what artifacts they're looking for because they've never actually seen them. They won't see them until they find and handle them. They know the basic shapes of the artifacts they're likely to find, but they don't know how the individual pieces will actually look. Will the chert flakes be gray or brown? Will the bottle glass be clear, brown, blue, yellow, or green? They know the patterns that fit the various mental pictures of "arrowhead," "scraper," "bottle neck," "dinner plate," and so forth, but that's all. They know that things called "arrowheads" should have pointed ends (if not broken), that they will be made of chipped stone (at pre-metal sites), and that they will conform to certain designs common for the region. Archaeologists have a framework for "stone tools" in mind, and they will pick up objects that have those general characteristics. Anything that does not fit into the mental image of "artifact" will not be picked up during the survey. A professional with a well-honed mental image of "arrowhead" can easily distinguish the real thing from a pointed rock. The lack of a well-developed mental framework for artifacts, in fact, is one reason why so many people take pieces of rocks and other nonartifacts to museums and universities for identification.

Even well-developed mental pictures can be fooled, however. While excavating colonial-era sites, I have sometimes mistaken white cigarette butts for the stems of white clay smoking pipes. From a distance, a cigarette butt visually fits the mental picture of "pipe stem": they are white in color, tube shaped, and approximately 1.5 inches (4 centimeters) long. Only when the butt is picked up is it clear that it violates an important feature of the mental framework: it must be made of kiln-fired white clay, not paper.

An artifact's shape is one of its most recognizable visual properties. Archaeologists conduct abduction when they infer the shape of an entire object from a single fragment. For instance, a historical archaeologist given a bottle neck and lip (technically called a "finish") with a square shape in cross section would immediately know that the piece is likely to have come from a nineteenth-century patent medicine bottle.

One advantage of this kind of recognition is that archaeologists can reasonably identify other pieces of the bottle because the shape of the other pieces can be inferred from the shape of the finish. The archaeologist has no need to fit all glass pieces to the finish by trial and error. The mental framework—developed through knowledge and experience—will do most of the work.

Archaeologists also regularly use visual abductive reasoning when they reconstruct buildings using the often-minimal evidence left behind, such as postholes and soil stains. Lines of postholes and the locations of wall trenches and hearths help them construct visual representations (often as computer models) that then can be constructed if desired. A number of experimental archaeologists have built life-sized models of ancient houses and then burned them down to assess how well the remains of the modern building conform to excavated physical remains. For example, archaeologists in the American Plains had the opportunity to compare the burned remains of an earthlodge excavated in Nebraska with a replica built in 1990 by the Mills County (Iowa) Historical Museum. When weather damaged the replica beyond repair, the museum decided to burn down its remains and construct a new one. The builders of the original replica had based it entirely on archaeological remains of lodges excavated in the region (a case of visual abduction). Once the replica was burned, archaeologists were able to compare its charred remains with those of the burned archaeological example in Nebraska.

The final form of an inductive argument with archaeological importance is "the argument by analogy." This form of argument is so widely used in archaeo-thinking that it deserves a chapter of its own.

Continue Reading

Archaeology

Bleed, Peter, Jerry Renaud, and Luis Peon-Casanova. 2009. Burning Issues: Observations on Old and New Burned Earthlodges. *Plains Anthropologist* 54: 19–25.

Deetz, James. 1965. *The Dynamics of Stylistic Change in Arikara Ceramics*. Urbana: University of Illinois Press.

Fagan, Brian M. 1987. *The Great Journey: The Peopling of Ancient America*. London: Thames and Hudson.

———. 2011. *The First North Americans: An Archaeological Journey*. London: Thames and Hudson.

Fladmark, K. R. 1979. Routes: Alternative Migration Corridors for Early Man in North America. *American Antiquity* 44: 55–69.

Misarti, Nicole, Bruce P. Finney, James W. Jordan, Herbert D. G. Maschner, Jason A. Addison, Mark D. Shapley, Andrea Krumhardt, and James E. Beget. 2012. Early Retreat of the Alaska Peninsula Glacier Complex and the Implications for Coastal Migrations of First Americans. *Quaternary Science Reviews* 48: 1–6.

Noël Hume, Ivor, and Henry M. Miller. 2011. Ivor Noël Hume: Historical Archaeologist. *The Public Historian* 33: 9–32.

Saraceni, Jessica E. 1996. Redating Serpent Mound. *Archaeology* 49, no. 6: 16.

Logic

Carroll, Lewis. 1896. *Symbolic Logic: Part I, Elementary*. London: Macmillan.

Salmon, Wesley C. 1973. *Logic*. 2nd ed. Englewood Cliffs, NJ: Prentice Hall.

Shelley, Cameron. 1996. Visual Abductive Reasoning in Archaeology. *Philosophy of Science* 63: 278–301.

Twain, Mark. 2010. *Autobiography of Mark Twain, Volume 1*. Edited by Harriet Elinor Smith. Berkeley: University of California Press.

Pseudo-Archaeology

Cremo, Michael A., and Richard L. Thompson. 1993. *Forbidden Archaeology: The Hidden History of the Human Race*. San Diego, CA: Bhaktivedanta Institute.

Donnelly, Ignatius. 1882. *Atlantis: The Antediluvian World*. New York: Harper and Brothers.

Fell, Barry. 1976. *America B.C.: Ancient Settlers in the New World*. New York: Demeter.

Menzies, Gavin. 2002. *1421: The Year China Discovered America*. New York: William Morrow.

Tyree, J. M. 2005. Ignatius Donnelly: Prince of Cranks. *The Believer* 3, no. 6: 5–14.

Is That Chair Really a Chair? **5**
Analogy and Archaeological Thinking

IKE MILLIONS OF PEOPLE around the world, I've always been fascinated by modern and contemporary art. But perhaps unlike connoisseurs, what has intrigued me the most is the artists' combination of skill, creativity, and audacity. One of the things I've found especially fascinating when thinking about contemporary art is the bewildered public's frequent question, "Why is *that* art?" I sometimes think what is accepted and admired often says more about the viewer than the artist. An artist's creativity can mean that decisions about what constitutes art may take a curious turn. This was exactly what happened to me.

A few years ago while visiting a famous art museum, I was confronted by what looked like a heavy wooden chair. It fit my mental framework of what a chair should be. It had four legs, a seat, and a back—nothing odd there. Its location, however, was confusing because it was placed in the middle of a room in the modern and contemporary art wing. This lead me to wonder, Was the chair art, or was it simply a chair? The object was not discreetly placed in one of the corners as a guard's chair might have been, out of the visitors' way yet near enough to monitor the exhibit. It was placed in the position of a sculpture.

My mind raced as I thought, This object certainly has all the characteristics of what I know a chair to be, but its placement in the gallery makes it seem like art. So, is it a chair, or is an artist using its apparent solidity and emptiness to reference some muted desire in the human spirit? Its appearance said "chair," but its location implied "art."

What exactly was going on? Why was I having this confusion, and what does it have to do with archaeo-thinking? The problem was that on entering the gallery and seeing the chair, my brain immediately and unconsciously made a simple analogy. The analogy, which took nanoseconds to compute but which resulted in confusion, was a calculation between my mental picture of "chair" (what I knew a chair to be) and "art" (what I suspected a piece of art could be). It was an analogy but not one I could easily resolve.

As Professor Stebbing tells us in *Thinking to Some Purpose*, analogies are one of the most widely used forms of inductive argument. Everyone uses them every day. Most of us usually make them so quickly and effortlessly that we don't even realize we're doing it. For example, when you walk into a classroom for the first time, your brain rapidly makes a simple analogy between what you know to exist elsewhere (chairs and desks in other classrooms) and what you see for the first time in the new setting (new chairs and desks). As you sit down, you are confident that your experience with similar objects in other places means you can safely sit on the new chairs without having them crumble beneath you. The context also helps you decide that the chairs can be sat on. In a classroom, your analogy is justifiably strong, but in the context of an art museum, I could not have the same confidence in my analogy. The "chair" I saw may have been made of papier-mâché. I would have made a fool of myself—and probably been arrested—had I attempted to sit in the "chair." (I never discovered the "chair's" true identity!)

An analogical argument takes the following form:

Objects of type X have attributes a, b, and c.
Objects of type Y have attributes a, b, and c.
Objects of type X have attribute d.
∴ Objects of type Y have attribute d.

During my experience at the art museum, I was trying to make this analogical argument:

Chairs have four legs, a seat, and a back.
The object in the gallery has four legs, a seat, and a back.
Chairs can be sat upon.
Therefore, the object in the gallery can be sat upon (?)

This is the same analogical argument you make every time you sit in a chair you have never seen before. If it has all the characteristics of a chair, it fits your mental picture of what a chair is, so you can safely sit on it. One pitfall, though, as Professor Stebbing says, is that we humans are often willing to accept any analogical comparison that seems to make sense without having to think too much about it. If it sounds good, we may accept it without evaluating its details. As we saw with my museum experience, such assumptions could have serious consequences!

Archaeologists and Analogy

Analogies, useful in daily life, are every bit as useful in archaeology. Amateur antiquarians, practicing their hobby before archaeology had become a professional discipline, used analogies when they first contemplated the monuments of ancient Egypt, Italy, and Europe. Many of their analogies were misguided and fanciful, and they would be easily discounted once archaeology was professionalized. But simple analogies constituted a significant element of early archaeological research.

When, in 1873, silver tycoon Heinrich Schliemann pulled out of the ground what he called "Priam's Treasure" at Troy, he described individual finds with the words "shield," "cup," "sauceboat," and "knife." These ancient objects probably never functioned in the ways Schliemann envisioned, but his analogies allowed the public to grasp their general shape and form. In fact, simply reading the words forces your brain to create an instantaneous visual image that makes each meaning (and thus function) clear. When we hear "shield," each of us quickly creates a mental image of how we think a shield should look.

While excavating the ancient ruins at Knossos in the early twentieth century, Arthur Evans used analogical reasoning to identify the "Grand Staircase" and the "Throne Room." The stairway and the room had the appearance of these things to him, he interpreted them that way, and his analogies helped others understand his interpretations. A big chair in one room looked to him like a throne, so its location became the "Throne Room." You probably have already created a picture of the room in your mind based on what you imagine a throne room to look like. Evans did the same thing (figure 5.1).

The use of analogies in archaeology continued to be informally used in this manner until about the 1960s. Since then, archaeologists have spent a great deal of time thinking about the importance of logical reasoning, and analogy—given its wide usage in archaeology—has been a natural topic.

When archaeologists started to think about it, they realized they make two kinds of analogies: *artifact analogies* and *cultural* or *ethnographic analogies*. Artifact analogies involve examining the shape and material of an artifact and associating it with something known from another source, either past

Figure 5.1.   Throne room at Knossos, Crete. Used by permission, The Ashmolean Museum, Oxford University.

or present. This is what Schliemann did with the artifacts from Troy. He saw what looked to him like a shield (he made a simple analogy) and gave the ancient artifact that functional name. Its past function (whether accurate or not) was thus clear to everyone.

Philosophers sometimes refer to Schliemann's shield analogy as a "single analogy" because the creator uses only one source. A cultural analogy is when an archaeologist uses ethnographic information to make an interpretation about archaeological remains in the broadest cultural sense. These analogies are considerably more complex than artifact analogies because, as "multiple analogies," they contain evidence from many sources. Cultural analogies are also complicated because they refer to cultural traditions and practices rather than to a single piece of material culture.

One of the most interesting features of artifact analogies is that they often include an implicit cultural analogy. This means that the similarities between two objects from different cultures can imply a similarity between the cultures themselves. A good example comes from one of the earliest recorded archaeological analogies.

Artifact Analogies

In 1699, Edward Lhwyd, the second Keeper of Oxford University's Ashmolean Museum, used an artifact analogy when he proposed that chipped stone artifacts found in prehistoric Scotland were used in the same way Native Americans employed similar-looking objects in seventeenth-century New England: as arrowheads. The residents of the rural Scottish Highlands, where Lhwyd's artifacts were found, believed the objects were charms created by elves and fairies, but Lhwyd used an analogy to dispute this interpretation:

> Stone artifacts found in Native New England are made of stone [a], they are chipped [b], generally triangular in shape [c], and pointed [d].
> Artifacts found in the Scottish Highlands have the characteristics a, b, c, and d.
> The artifacts in North America are employed as arrowheads [e].
> Therefore, the artifacts in Scotland were used as arrowheads [e].

In this example, Lhwyd infers the artifact's *function* from its *form*. The Scottish artifacts looked like those used in North America, so they probably had the same function. The link between form and function is common in archaeological analogies.

Archaeologists studying non- or preliterate societies from the distant past face the problem noted by philosopher Marilee Salmon: "There is obviously no opportunity to question the makers of these artifacts about their purposes in designing them." Also, not being ethnographers, archaeologists cannot see these objects being put to use. They must use analogies to infer their use from their form. Archaeologists know, for instance, that an arrowhead cannot be used to carry drinking water. This is an easy conclusion to make. But difficulty comes from attempting to decide whether an arrowhead may have had a purely symbolic meaning or was simply used in hunting or warfare. Form relates to function but not necessarily in every case.

Historical archaeologists and ethnoarchaeologists (archaeologists working as ethnographers among living communities) often have opportunities to question the makers and users of artifacts, and past function can often be inferred from direct, personal knowledge. The artifacts excavated from a late nineteenth-century farmhouse site, for example, may not be entirely unfamiliar to an archaeologist today. Some objects might be unfamiliar, but most of them—ceramic plates, porcelain cups, wooden dominoes, brass buttons, and glass bottles—will be easily recognizable. Even so, no guarantee exists that the form of an object will match the expected function. The symbolic use of four-hole buttons is an excellent example (see chapter 3). "Witch bottles" are another intriguing case in point.

British archaeologists excavating at seventeenth- and eighteenth-century house sites sometimes find glass and stoneware bottles containing human hair, urine, iron nails, nail clippings, and cloth hearts pierced with straight pins (figure 5.2). The bottles, clearly once functioning as liquid containers, in the end were used for magic. Superstitious people used such bottles as charms to drive away witches and to promote better health. The form of the witch bottle is quite familiar today (as a container), but its final function (as a charm) is completely foreign to us.

Writers of fringe archaeology are prone to making artifact analogies in the attempt to increase the plausibility of their shaky interpretations. Their outra-

Figure 5.2. Witch bottle found at Holywell Priory, London. Used by permission, Museum of London Archaeology (Photo: Andy Chopping).

geous examples are instructive because one doesn't generally need a great deal of knowledge to evaluate them. You need only a dose of common sense.

Barry Fell, in *America, B.C.*, makes an analogy between a form of ancient European writing called "ogham" and various scratches found on rocks in North America. Ogham is an ancient Irish writing system dating to the first millennium CE. Instead of appearing as a script, ogham is composed of a series of horizontal and diagonal lines extending from or crossing over a vertical line (figure 5.3). A few examples can still be found in rural Ireland, where their presence makes perfect sense. Fell, however, identified scratches found on rocks in the United States as ogham and argued that Celtic people from the Old World came to the eastern United States long before Columbus. His analogy is as follows:

Ogham writing consists of a vertical line [*a*] and a series of horizontal [*b*] and diagonal lines [*c*].

Rocks with characteristics a, b, and c appear in the eastern United States.

Ogham writing was the product of ancient Irish Celts [d].

Burnfort Ogham.

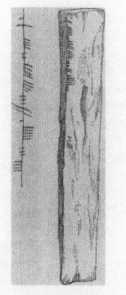
Glounaclough Ogham

Figure 5.3. Ogham writing on two standing stones in Ireland. From John Windele, "Ogham Inscriptions," *Transactions of the Kilkenny Archaeological Society*, vol. 1, 1850.

Therefore, the scratched rocks in the US were made by ancient Irish Celts [d].

His analogy is extremely weak and, most professional archaeologists would say, ridiculous. To evaluate his analogy, we need only ask a few simple questions:

1. Are the scratch marks on rocks in the United States really ogham writing or just scratch marks?
2. Do the U.S. scratch marks date to the first millennium CE?
3. Is there any concrete archaeological evidence for Celtic presence in pre-Columbian America?
4. Does any evidence exist to prove that ancient Celts knew about the Western Hemisphere? and, if so,
5. Does any evidence show they had interest in visiting it?

Without archaeological evidence, Fell's analogy rests strictly on supposition. It is the weakest kind of artifact analogy because what could be simpler than comparing straight lines?

Cultural Analogies

Cultural, or ethnographic, analogies are usually "multiple analogies." These analogies can often be more difficult to evaluate than single-source analogies. The increase in the amount of information can strengthen an analogy but only if the information is consistent and complementary. Cultural information extracted from widely different cultures can weaken an analogy, leaving it open to criticism.

Archaeologists use two kinds of ethnographic analogies: *historical* and *comparative*. Both have been around for a long time, and both continue to serve archaeo-thinkers as they struggle to interpret the past. Here, the historical analogy is represented by the direct historical approach and the comparative analogy by the ethnographic analogy.

As noted in chapter 1, early nineteenth-century antiquarians constructed analogies to interpret the earthen mounds of North America. Assuming that Native Americans were incapable of building such massive structures, the antiquarians created analogies using the barrows of Europe, the pyramids of Egypt, or some invented culture. By the end of the nineteenth century and certainly by the start of the twentieth, most archaeologists had abandoned the use of extremely weak analogies, seeking instead to understand culture change as exhibited in artifact deposits. Out of this interest developed what American archaeologists call "the direct historical approach." (Europeans call it "the Folk Culture approach.")

The Direct Historical Approach

The idea behind the direct historical approach is simple. The idea underlying it maintains that archaeologists can infer characteristics of the unknown (an ancient, undocumented archaeological culture) from the known (an observable or historically documented culture). The direction of analysis thus moves from the ethnographic present (the date of a written account or observation) to the archaeological past (the dates of the settlement being studied). Using attributes compiled as "trait lists," the analyst simply compares the elements of the ethnographic culture with those of the next-closest archaeological culture (in terms of date), moving step-by-step backward in time until an entire culture history is constructed.

The direct historical approach can be further explained with a simplified hypothetical example (table 5.1). This example is an ethnographic account of a culture that wears shell beads, cooks in red pots, lives in round houses, uses iron scrapers to prepare hides, and travels on rivers with canoes. The date of the fictional account is 1770–1775, and its author is a Jesuit missionary. The first archeological site (A) in the example dates to 1650–1700, or not long before the visitor reached the village and wrote about it. The excavation of Site A unearthed shell beads, red pots, and postholes for round-shaped houses. The archaeologists found no evidence of canoes and no iron scrapers. They did find chipped stone scrapers, however. Based on the history of

Table 5.1. The Direct Historical Approach in Action

	Ethnographic 1770–1775	Archaeological Sites			
		A (1650–1700)	B (1500–1600)	C (1400–1500)	D (1300–1350)
Attributes					
Shell beads	x	x	x	x	
Red pots	x	x			
Round houses	x	x	x		
Metal scrapers	x				
Canoes	x				
Stone beads					x
Black pots			x	x	x
Square houses				x	x
Chert scrapers		x	x	x	x

European colonization in the region, the archaeologists conclude that European traders introduced the iron scrapers at the time of first meeting the villagers. According to fairly reliable map, the encounter between the cultures occurred in August 1760. The stone scrapers, which predate the iron ones, were probably how the villagers traditionally prepared their animal hides. The archaeological culture at Site B (1500–1600) had the same attributes as Culture A, except that they used black pots in place of red ones. In Culture C (1400–1500), the archaeologists discovered that the people had much the same material culture as Culture B, except that they had lived in square houses. In archaeological Culture D, the excavators learned that about 100 years earlier (1300–1350) the people wore stone beads, used stone scrapers and black pots exclusively, and lived in square houses.

Two key elements are important to take away from this simple example. First, the process allows archaeologists to move steadily and systematically backward in time to frame analogies between each of the individual cultural expressions, beginning with the one visited by the missionary. A second thing to note is that the material culture of Culture D (1300–1350) does not look anything like that of the ethnographic culture (1770–1775) even though they were culturally related. Using the direct historical approach, archaeologists can make a direct connection between the two, even though they are distant in time between 420 and 475 years, (depending on the beginning or end dates of occupation). Four hundred years is a long time, and we can see cultural change reflected in the material things the people used over this period.

The direct historical approach, though a useful form of cultural analogy, has two major weaknesses. First and most significant, the approach appears to reduce cultures to stationary, snapshot images rather than constantly changing cultural expressions. Cultures adapt and invent, and no single picture can capture the richness and diversity of any culture throughout its entire history. This is why archaeologists study several sites: they hope to be able to learn something about cultural changes through time. The direct historical approach provides this level of analysis, but only by appreciating that gaps in time may occur between the occupational periods represented by each site. In the example, culture change continued to occur during the time gaps between each site's period of occupation even if archaeologists cannot see it. It is hoped that further research, over time, will fill in the gaps between the sites.

A second problem with the direct historical approach is that it works best in places where the cultures have not moved around too much. A lack of migration increases the reliability of the between-site analogies. Archaeologists may not be able to establish connections between an ethnographic observation and earlier archaeological remains when a great deal of migration has occurred. In the example, it may be that Culture D is not culturally related to the ethnographic culture at all or perhaps even to Cultures A, B, or C. Perhaps the people in Culture D faced a drought and moved hundreds of miles away from their homeland and between 1350 and 1400 another culture occupied their former territory. This would account for the difference between the material expressions of Cultures C and D; the remains represent two distinct cultures rather than an example of cultural evolution.

Ethnographic Analogy

Archaeo-thinkers face considerable challenges when attempting to use comparative ethnographic analogies because they require controlling more variables than the simple trait lists of the direct historical approach. Greater sophistication in archaeology since the late twentieth century means that archaeologists cannot investigate culture change with trait lists alone. No longer can they simply list two cultures' material traits, check the traits against one another, and conclude that a historical connection existed between the cultures. Today's ethnographic analogies require amassing a body of reliable information that will help archaeologists interpret the complex cultural traditions and practices of history. Even so, however, the pitfalls can increase with the number of sources used because the archaeologist must ensure the reliability of each source.

A well-known archaeological example of the use of cultural analogies is Lewis Binford's "Smudge Pits and Hide Smoking: The Use of Analogy in Archaeological Reasoning," published in 1967. This study was largely responsible for making archaeologists aware of the use of analogies in archaeology while at the same time exposing the need for extreme care in using them.

While excavating at the precontact Toothsome Site in central Illinois, Binford discovered 15 pit features, each with the same general characteristics. Each was slightly oval in shape and only about 12 inches (30.5 centimeters) in length and width. The bottom of each pit was filled with charred twigs, corncobs, and other fibers. The people who dug these pits had placed them at random around the site's three buildings.

Reading the reports of fellow archaeologists, Binford learned that many others had discovered similar pits in their own excavations. These archaeologists usually described the pits as "caches" or "corncob pits" and said little else. Binford wanted a more culturally sensitive interpretation, one that would provide insight into the daily lives of the people who had lived in the small village. He wanted to know what about their culture caused them to make and use the pits. To provide a culturally relevant interpretation, Binford created an analogical argument to interpret the pits' past functions.

Binford's ethnographic survey revealed that at least four Native American cultures in the American Southeast, five from the Plains, and three from the Great Lakes region had all used shallow pits to tan hides. Various observers had seen native peoples lighting smoky fires in the pits and then stretching hides over the holes to darken them and to help preserve them from insects. The visitors' descriptions of the pits matched those at the Toothsome Site reasonably well, so Binford concluded, based on this evidence, that the 15 pits he found had probably been used in the hide-smoking process. Even though Binford started with the archaeological evidence, his ethnographic analogy can be written as follows:

Pits indentified in various ethnographic accounts are small [a], oval [b], and contain charred materials [c].
The 15 pits found at the Toothsome Site are small [a], oval [b], and contain charred materials [c].
The ethnographic pits functioned to darken hides [d].
Therefore, the Toothsome Site pits had been used to darken hides [d].

This is a straightforward analogical argument made between ethnographic descriptions and archaeologically discovered material culture. It allowed Binford to infer an otherwise unrecognized cultural practice (hide smoking) from excavated physical remains.

Evaluating Analogy Strength

Binford's article was an immediate sensation among archaeologists, and it quickly brought the subject of analogy to the forefront of archaeo-thinking. But it was controversial. Only two years after the article appeared, archaeologist Patrick Munson offered another interpretation of the pits. Using a different set of ethnographies to create his own analogy, Munson demonstrated that the residents of the Toothsome Site may have used the pits for smudging the insides of clay pots rather than for (or perhaps in addition to) smoking animal hides. Archaeologists excavating Native American village sites in the American Southeast—the only region from which Munson drew his ethnographic information and the area that archaeologists considered most closely related to the people who inhabited the Toothsome Site—had found sherds with blackened interiors. Munson thus presented an alternative claim: that native potters produced blackened pot interiors using the small, shallow pits.

The ethnographic information Munson presented raised an important question about the archaeological use of analogy: how do archaeologists know which analogy is the best one? To put it more formally, how do we determine the *relevance* or *applicability* of an analogy? Is it the right one for the situation or has the archaeologist stretched the analogy too far? In the effort to "make the case," did the archaeologist choose only ethnographic examples that suited his or her interpretation?

Some questions can be answered by taking a closer look at Binford's sources, by evaluating them based on what I call the TST test: the time, space, and technology test. The relevant information to consider is how well the ethnographic sources match the archaeological case along these three dimensions.

Regarding time, the Toothsome Site residents were part of what archaeologists broadly term the Mississippian Culture. The dates for this culture range from about 700 to about 1600 CE depending on location, with the villages in the region of the Toothsome Site dating to around 1000–1500 CE. If these historical dates are placed alongside Binford's sources, we can see the problem immediately (table 5.2). The dates of his ethnographic sources are hundreds of years later than the Toothsome Site dates. The minimum mean dates are 352 years apart, with the maximum discrepancy between the dates being a whopping 896 years. Even if we accept the minimum discrepancy

Table 5.2.   Date Differences between the Toothsome Site and the Ethnographic Sources

Toothsome Site	Ethnographic Dates	Minimum Difference (years)	Maximum Difference (years)
1000–1500	1700–1750	200	750
	1900–1950	400	950
	1900–1950	400	950
	1900–1950	400	950
	1850–1900	350	900
	1800–1850	300	850
	1850–1900	350	900
	1800–1850	300	850
	1900–1939	400	939
	1850–1860	350	860
	1800–1890	300	890
	1930–1940	430	940
	1900–1920	400	920
	Mean	352	896

of just over 350 years, we must still resolve a number of cultural implications because of the number of assumptions we would also have to make.

The most serious assumption is that the ethnographic cultures Binford used did not experience any significant changes in how they prepared hides for at least 200 years, or between about 1500 (the final date when people lived at the Toothsome Site) and 1700 (the date of his earliest written source). In other words, the hide-smoking activities the observers directly witnessed were the same as those the Toothsome Site residents had practiced long before. This is a huge assumption to make in light of the significant technological and ecological impacts Europeans made throughout Native North America.

Regarding space, if we compare the location of the Toothsome Site and the locations in Binford's sample of ethnographic cultures, we can also see large discrepancies (table 5.3). None of the cultures lived especially close to the Toothsome Site. None of them lived in Illinois or even in states bordering Illinois. The exception is the Menominis, but even they lived far away in northern Wisconsin, a distance of about 500 miles (805 kilometers) from Binford's site.

In terms of technology, the strongest analogies derived from comparing cultures that manipulated the environment in roughly similar ways using comparable technologies. For example, it would make little sense to use an industrial market economy in an analogy with a culture of hunters and collectors, even if the criteria of time and space could be managed. The

Table 5.3.   Place Differences between the Toothsome Site
and the Ethnographic Sources

Culture	Place
Toothsome Site	South-central Illinois
Natchez	Mississippi, Louisiana
Creek	Alabama, Georgia, Oklahoma
Choctaw	Mississippi, Oklahoma
Seminole	Florida, Oklahoma
Omaha	Nebraska
Dakota	Minnesota, South Dakota
Blackfoot	Montana, Alberta
Crow	Montana
Arapaho	Colorado, Nebraska, Kansas
Iroquois	New York State
Ojibwa	Northern Michigan, Ontario
Menomini	Northeastern Wisconsin

cultural practices in such wildly diverse cultures may allow for the creation of an analogy that initially may seem reasonable but is actually misguided.

Technology is a much more difficult variable to assess because many of the ethnographic cultures Binford used in his analogy were horticultural peoples just like the residents of the Toothsome Site. A major deficiency appears, however, when considering the dates of the observations in conjunction with technology. With the exception of the Natchez, the dates of all the ethnographies belong to eras long after the native cultures had adopted many Western ways. For example, the Creeks, Choctaws, and Seminoles were members of the so-called Five Civilized Tribes, cultures forcibly evicted from their homes in the American Southeast and moved to the Oklahoma Territory in the 1830s. Nineteenth-century Americans referred to them as "civilized" because they had begun to accept many European ways, including Western styles of dress, animal-powered agriculture, log cabins, and a form of enslavement. A creative Cherokee man even invented a written transcription for their spoken language, and the people used it to print a Cherokee newspaper. Writing about the Seminoles living in Oklahoma, anthropologist Richard Sattler noted that "Western Seminole culture in the nineteenth century generally conformed to pre-Removal Seminole and Creek patterns, but twentieth-century conditions produced profound changes." The accounts of these cultures Binford used date to 1900–1950, decades after they had been removed. The source he used, Alanson Skinner's 1913 report among the Florida Seminoles—those who had not been removed—indicates that members of the eastern band had maintained many of their traditional practices. While this seems to strengthen their presence in Binford's analogy, Skinner did note that many of the band regularly visited Miami and Fort Lauderdale to trade. Thus, while they were indeed located in a remote area, they were not unconnected to or uninfluenced by Western ways. By the same token, when other ethnographers made their observations, some of the cultures (namely, the Dakotas, Blackfoots, Crows, and Arapahoes) were not horticulturalists at all but horse-riding hunters. Their nomadic way of life would have been completely foreign to the sedentary residents of the Toothsome Site.

Based on the TST test, Binford's analogy ascribing the Toothsome Site's pit features to the process of smoking hides appears shaky. So, how might we improve it? The ideal situation, of course, would be to find eyewitness accounts from the first literate visitors, individuals who could have observed the native cultures before the impacts of foreign diseases altered them forever. Such information would provide greater confidence along the dimension of space. We would have less confidence in the technological dimension because of cultural change, but the analogy would still be strengthened. The dimension of time would present a problem, but the difference in years would roughly match that of the Natchez in the original analogy (approximately a 200- to 750-year difference). We might be able to live with this time span, but it would always be problematic.

Archaeologists investigating ancient cultures will always have difficulty along the temporal dimension when they attempt to devise analogical arguments. So, how might we create stronger analogies, ones that include a closer agreement in time? The answer comes from historical archaeology.

Exploring the role of analogy in historical archaeology, Robert Schuyler presented the case of three iron artifacts archaeologists had excavated at the eighteenth-century Fortress of Louisbourg in Nova Scotia, Canada. French colonists had begun to build a small village on the site in 1713, and when they were finished, they had constructed a fortified city much like those that dotted the landscapes of continental Europe. The thick, stone walls of the city made a political statement that was difficult to misinterpret: Louisbourg was an important outpost of France's colonial North American empire, and they took its defense seriously. Understanding the statement very well—and appreciating the strategic importance of the location—the British, France's longtime enemies, attacked the city twice. They finally destroyed the fortress in the 1760s after they had defeated France in the Seven Years' War. The archaeology there, begun in 1959, is one of the world's flagship examples of French colonial archaeology.

The Louisbourg archaeologists realized that the iron artifacts had been designed to be affixed to wooden handles like a broom or a rake. This interpretation made sense, but the form of the objects was unusual: each one appeared as a set of twisted tines. The three specimens were each of a different size. Their archaeological contexts made it clear that they were French artifacts dating to the eighteenth century, but how they had been used was a mystery.

Seeking to find an answer, Schuyler checked a source called *Encyclopédie*, written in 1762 by French scholar Denis Diderot. He discovered that these objects, well known in the eighteenth century, were called *tirebourre* (figure 5.4). The objects were fixed to long wooden handles as the archaeologists had surmised, but they had a specialized function, one that would be unknown to most people alive today.

In the eighteenth century, artillery soldiers shoved tirebourre down the mouths of cannons to extract the cotton wad they had pushed down the muzzle to fire the previous cannonball. When a shot misfired, the soldiers

Figure 5.4.   Tirebourres from Fortress Louisbourg, Nova Scotia, Canada. Top: 1B16C3-141; center: 1L1X3-5, 51L3H2-5; bottom: 1B1E11-456. Courtesy Parks Canada/Heidi Moses/9298E. Photograph by Heidi Moses.

had to unload the cannon, an operation that included removing the wad of cotton as well. For the next shot, they were afraid to use the old wad because, if smoldering, it could explode and kill them all. Thus, they used the tirebourre, an extremely valuable tool!

The case of the tirebourre shows that the construction of a perfect analogy is possible in archaeology. Schuyler's analogy between Diderot's encyclopedia and the three Louisbourg artifacts meets the challenge of the TST test. The analogy is perfect in terms of time (both the objects and the source belong to the eighteenth century; in fact, they are contemporaneous), space (cultural rather than geographic space; France and a colonial French outpost modeled on the Old Country), and technology (they are part of the same European society). Such one-to-one analogies, what Schuyler termed "historic analogs," are the tightest analogies archaeologists can construct.

What Is the Purpose of Analogy in Archaeology?

Not all archaeologists have accepted the application of analogical reasoning in archaeology. Some archaeologists studying very ancient societies believe that the time gap is simply too great between the cultures they study and the accounts written by much-later observers. They say that cultural change is too prevalent a force in human history to give the analogies much merit when so much time has elapsed.

These archaeologists are correct, and their position can be appreciated by thinking about the fast pace of change in our own time. Only a few years ago, the idea of a handheld computer existed only in science fiction. Today, we take these things for granted. They are so familiar that we don't even call them tiny computers; we call them smart phones. Just think about the changes these little tools have brought about in our daily lives. Our digital age might be a wholly unique example because of the speed of change, but anthropologists know that all cultures constantly change wherever they are (in space) and whenever they lived (in time).

As noted in the hypothetical example of the direct historical approach, the contacts that may have occurred between different cultures raise problems when equating the ethnographic present with the archaeological past. The influence of cultural change as a result of outside influence may have transformed the ethnographic culture in ways completely inconsistent with the archaeological culture. Some archaeologists worry that selecting only a few comparative attributes from a multicultural complex may provide misleading analogies. Years of research into the complex variability of cultural change has led some archeologists to conclude that ethnographic analogy is just too simple a method to explain complicated cultural history.

Many archaeologists, however, continue to think that analogy must play a role in archaeo-thinking. After all, even though Munson showed that the pits at the Toothsome Site may have been used for darkening pots rather than hides, Binford's basic point—that the pits were probably used for smoking *something*—stands up. Without analogy, archaeologists may not have recognized the ancient practice of smudging at long-abandoned village sites for many years. Skeptics may counter that a clever archaeologist may have devised this interpretation without using an analogy, and that may well be true. But one important value of the analogy is that it helps humanize the pits by allowing analysts to envision real people using them. The addition of ethnographic writings, made by observers watching people practice their cultural lives, helps to breathe life into dry archaeological specimens.

One of the most controversial aspects of the archaeological use of ethnographic analogies concerns whether they are useful for devising new ideas to test or whether they are best used for testing ideas that have already been formulated. In other words, do analogies help archaeologists think up new propositions, or are they good only for testing the ones they already have?

Archaeologists have had trouble answering this question. A general consensus is that analogical reasoning is fine when archaeologists use specific historical analogies rather than general comparative ones. Regardless of how they choose to use analogy, archaeologists must always be careful not to make bad analogies. These are often far too easy to create, and the thoughtful archaeo-thinker must always be on the lookout for them.

Another problem exists with poorly framed analogies. To understand this, let's return to the artifact analogy Lhywd presented in 1699.

Implicit in Lhywd's analogy is the idea that the similar use of arrows (and thus bows) suggests that the cultures of seventeenth-century Native Americans and prehistoric Scots might have been similar as well. Hidden within his artifact analogy is a subtle cultural analogy. To appreciate the significance of this, we must understand the cultural context of late seventeenth-century history.

New England, the American region undoubtedly most familiar to Lhywd, was the scene of unresolved conflicts between indigenous residents and European newcomers. In 1699, the Pequot War, the first sustained English–Indian armed conflict on the continent, had occurred only about 60 years earlier, and King Philip's War was only about 40 years in the past. The English–Native conflicts occurring during King William's War (1689–1697) were only two years distant. Alliances between French Canadian colonists and their Native allies to the north kept the British in New England up at night. In addition, thousands of Native peoples lived west of the mountains that defined the original English colonies. Many of these cultures would have their own battles with British and American settlers in the future.

At the same time, relations between Scotland and England were also tense, and the political union between the two would come only eight years after Lhywd made his analogy (in 1707). Tensions between England and Scotland were still tense 100 years later. The Highland Clearances, the eviction of hundreds of rural families from their land in an effort to "improve" them, occurred during the eighteenth and nineteenth centuries. During this long history, many English men and women believed the Scots to be culturally backward. The only way to help them "better" themselves was to make them more English. Most English men and women had the same attitude about New England native peoples; they simply needed to be more English.

With this cultural and historical backdrop, it may be that Lhywd's analogy carried with it a concealed message. He may have thought that Highland Scots and American Indians, both of whom were in direct, long-term contact with English men and women, were equally savage. And being so, each needed to be brought under the civilizing umbrella of the expanding British Empire. Equating an ancient European people (the ancient Scots) with living American cultures also implied that Native Americans were stuck in a time warp. Living American Indians lived just like ancient Europeans, and, given the then-understood laws of cultural evolution, New England's Indians had not progressed up the cultural ladder.

The idea that Lhywd's analogy may contain a hidden message proves Professor Stebbing's point that we must proceed cautiously when accepting any analogy, particularly one equating cultures. Like everything else in archaeological thinking, the use of analogies requires thought and consideration. An entire interpretation about the past can be smashed to pieces with a weak, misleading, or just plain bad analogy. Part of the difficulty of assessing the relevance of an analogy arises because, as Wesley Salmon notes in *Logic*, the strength of an analogy cannot be determined with formal logic alone. Once we understand the proper form of an analogical argument, the rest is up to us. We must use our knowledge to create sensible analogies just as we must use care when evaluating the analogies of others. We must be on the lookout for bad analogies as we learn to think like archaeologists.

The direct historical approach and the use of ethnographic analogies show that archaeologists regularly rely on written sources of information. Although archaeologists are interested mostly in understanding the relationships between humans and the things with which our ancestors surrounded themselves, every archaeologist must consult a variety of written materials when conducting research. Since archaeologists are not historians, how do they know what sources to trust, and why is the understanding of written sources important for archaeo-thinkers? The next chapter seeks to answer these questions.

Continue Reading

Archaeological Analogy

Diderot, Denis. 1993 [1751–1772]. *Diderot Pictorial Encyclopedia of Trades and Industry*. 2 vols. New York: Dover.

Evans, Arthur. 1921. *The Palace of Minos: A Comparative Account of the Successive Stages of the Early Cretan Civilization as Illustrated by the Discoveries at Knossos, Volume 1*. London: Macmillan.

Merrifield, Ralph. 1988. *The Archaeology of Ritual and Magic*. New York: New Amsterdam.

Sattler, Richard A. 2004. Seminole in the West. In *Handbook of North American Indians, Vol. 14: Southeast*, edited by Raymond D. Fogelson, 450–64. Washington, DC: Smithsonian Institution Press.

Schliemann, Heinrich. 1875. *Troy and Its Remains: A Narrative of Researches and Discoveries Made on the Site of Ilium and in the Trojan Plain.* Edited by Philip Smith. London: John Murray.

Skinner, Alanson. 1913. Notes on the Florida Seminole. *American Anthropologist* 15: 63–77.

Theory of Archaeological Analogy

Binford, Lewis. 1967. Smudge Pits and Hide Smoking: The Use of Analogy in Archaeological Reasoning. *American Antiquity* 32: 1–12.

Lyman, R. Lee, and Michael J. O'Brien. 2001. The Direct Historical Approach, Analogical Reasoning, and Theory in Americanist Archaeology. *Journal of Archaeological Method and Theory* 8: 303–42.

Munson, Patrick J. 1969. Comments on Binford's "Smudge Pits and Hide Smoking: The Use of Analogy in Archaeological Reasoning." *American Antiquity* 34: 83–85.

Salmon, Merrilee H. 1982. *Philosophy and Archaeology.* New York: Academic Press.

Schuyler, Robert L. 1968. The Use of Historic Analogs in Archaeology. *American Antiquity* 33: 390–92.

Shelley, Cameron. 1999. Multiple Analogies in Archaeology. *Philosophy of Science* 66: 579–605.

Wolverton, Steve, and R. Lee Lyman. 2000. Immanence and Configuration in Analogical Reasoning. *North American Archaeologist* 21: 233–47.

Wylie, Alison. 1985. The Reaction against Analogy. In *Advances in Archaeological Method and Theory*, vol. 8, edited by Michael Brian Schiffer, pp. 63–111. New York: Academic Press.

Source-Thinking 6
The Relationship between
Archaeological and Textual Evidence

I S ARCHAEOLOGY HISTORY? This question, so late in the book, may surprise you. You may have an answer ready. On the other hand, perhaps you've never thought about it, having assumed that the answer is obvious. Archaeologists study the past, and the past is history—it's that simple. Or is it?

Chapter 3 presents some information about the relationship between archaeology and history in explaining the difference between past actuality and chronicle. How archaeologists should think about history is a more profound issue, however. Central concerns are how archaeologists choose to define history and, once defined, what sources they deem appropriate to use.

What Is History?
History has many meanings, and three are relevant to archaeological research. First, history can refer to all time "in the past." "Past" in this case means all time before the particular moment you read this sentence. What you did yesterday is now part of history, and it belongs to past actuality. The *Oxford English Dictionary* (*OED*) defines this sense of history as "the aggregate of past events in general." History is simply "what has happened." A second meaning of history can refer to the academic discipline pursued by men and women who are identified as historians. The *OED* defines this meaning as "that branch of knowledge which deals with past events." A third meaning of "history" has been the most archaeologically important one. It has also become the most controversial one because it equates history with writing.

In classic archaeological thinking, "history" began with writing, and "prehistory" (literally, the time before "history") is all the time that existed before the advent of writing. James Deetz, whom we met in chapter 5, was explicit about this widely accepted meaning in *Invitation to Archaeology*: "Prehistory treats the time before man learned to write and therefore record his own career on earth. It begins with man's first appearance on this planet, almost two million years ago, and usually ends with the beginnings of written history in all parts of the world." This concept of archaeological time first gained expression in 1851, and it has remained in place until recently.

Beginning around 2000, a number of archaeologists observed that the prehistory/history divide was deficient in two important ways. First, it created an artificial break in time. People living in "prehistory" didn't wake up one day and realize they were suddenly "historic" because people with a written system of communication had arrived among them. Based on this obvious situation, some archaeologists argued that history flows in an unbroken number of days and seasons and that any division of time is arbitrary. Their reasoning makes a great deal of sense because we all experience history this way. Second, and much more damning, is the idea that the prehistory/history divide implies either that people without writing do not have history or that they are somehow less intelligent than people with writing. Anthropologist Eric Wolf, in his renowned *Europe and the People without History*, consciously used the idea of "lacking history" to highlight the ways in which "'primitives,' peasantries, laborers, immigrants, and besieged minorities" have been ignored in the written chronicles of the dominant classes. Thus, the problem with the prefix "pre" in prehistory is that it can also signify "primitive," a point Wolf understood by putting the word in quotes.

The use and meaning of the prehistory/history divide is still being debated. To get around the problem, many archaeologists have ceased using "prehistory" and now use "precontact" to refer to the time before indigenous peoples encountered colonizing Europeans. After all, "pre" history is still history; it constitutes part of past actuality no matter what we choose to call it. The unavoidable conclusion, then, is simply that archaeologists study human history—from the beginning to the present day.

Regardless of how we wish to think about the broad sweep of time and how we might carve it up for analytical reasons, the use of written sources of information, as we saw with the ethnographic analogies discussed in chapter 5, are a necessary part of archaeo-thinking. The analysis of written accounts is as much a part of archaeological research as is the examination of artifacts, building remains, plant seeds, and other materials. Given the importance of textual sources, does the study of documents make archaeologists historians? Or do archaeologists look for different things in documents than historians? These important questions require archaeo-thinking because they directly concern how individual archaeologists perceive what it is they do.

Archaeology and History

After the 1960s, American archaeologists began to feel ill at ease thinking about themselves as historians. Before then, many called themselves "culture historians," meaning that their goal was to construct the history of nonliterate cultures. But in the late 1960s, with the rise of processual archaeology (see chapter 1), American archaeologists tended to move away from specifically thinking about history. One reason was that they were usually (though not always) trained in departments of anthropology. (Archaeologists specializing in classical, Egyptian, and biblical archaeology have much less difficulty thinking of themselves as historians because they are usually trained in departments of history, classics, or even ancient languages.) The anthropological concentration in American archaeological training means that individual archaeologists tend to have various degrees of exposure to historical analysis. Some are well grounded in historical analysis, while others may have little or no training in it at all. This was not always the case, however.

Between 1900 and about 1965, many scholars characterized American anthropology as "historical anthropology." Students of this intellectual tradition collected vast amounts of cultural and historical information from America's living indigenous peoples. Their goal was to document as much as they could before the traditions disappeared forever. The job of like-minded archaeologists was to construct the deep histories of the same peoples using artifacts and the remains of their ancient settlements, hence the term "culture historian." But as archaeologists struggled to find their scientific voice in the 1960s and early 1970s, many of them left historical analysis behind, viewing it as unscientific. During this era of transformation, many different kinds of scholars, including archaeologists, sought to graft many of the methods and perspectives of the hard sciences onto the social sciences and the humanities.

The debate over history versus science was especially complex in historical archaeology because the word "historical" was in the discipline's name. Archaeologists interested in post–1500 CE (post-Columbian) cultures debated whether they were "historical archaeologists" or "archaeological historians." By the late twentieth century, most American archaeologists had concluded that their research involved the past no matter how they perceived it, and most forgot about the controversy.

Surprisingly, historians went through the same period of introspection. Books with some variation of the title *What Is History?* became common. The books' authors typically struggle to describe what the profession of history actually seeks to accomplish. The era of experimentation linking their discipline to the hard sciences produced cliometrics, the study of the past using numerical data, number crunching, and multivariate statistics. The link between history and the humanities in turn led to psychohistory, an attempt to understand the hidden motivations of past historical actors using psychoanalysis and other methods adapted from psychology. Beginning in the late twentieth century and continuing into the twenty-first, a number of historians have debated the pros and cons of global or world history (macrohistory) as opposed to the history of the small (microhistory). Microhistory is the close examination of a single person or community's life in the hope that it may shed light on larger social and cultural issues. Global history involves the examination of worldwide trends and intercontinental patterns of action.

Regardless of how an archaeologist wishes to describe him- or herself in relation to the study of the past, all archaeologists must study written documents at some point during their careers. Where archaeology is concerned, a useful rule of thumb is this: *the further one goes back in time, the fewer documents exist to be studied; the more recent a site's date, the greater the number and diversity of textual sources.* Archaeologists investigating cultures living thousands of years ago may be restricted to reading the reports of other archaeologists and possibly the accounts of one or two explorers who visited the region and wrote down their impressions. Contemporary documents will not exist, and only the occasional petroglyph, cave painting, or carving may be available. An archaeologist examining an eighteenth-century colonial outpost may have an abundance of textual sources to read, including maps, letters, diaries, governmental reports, and inventories. Someone researching a late nineteenth-century urban townhouse will have even more records to sift through.

Regardless of how one feels about the relationship between archaeology and history—and most twenty-first-century archaeologists readily agree that they study history even if they use high-tech equipment, chemical testing, and dense scientific jargon—archaeologists have learned from historians that they need to know something about how to evaluate a diverse variety of sources in addition to the artifacts, buried features, settlement remains, and other materials they already know how to analyze.

The general public tends to perceive archaeologists as excavating explorers rather than as archive-bound historians, and this image is true to an extent. Archaeologists spend a great deal of time outdoors crawling into caves, walking hillsides, and combing through soil. But an archaeologist is just as likely to be found in an archive sitting alongside a historian or a genealogist. As a result, good archaeological thinkers know how to evaluate the kinds of sources generally associated with "historians" but also used by archaeologists.

"Historical" Sources

Imagining that professional historians study only written sources, many people may envision them sitting in wood-paneled archives hunched over piles of yellowed documents furiously typing on laptops or jotting down notes. This image is correct. Historians do sit for hours in archives and libraries, thumbing through boxes of old manuscripts. Many past historians commonly thought of written records as their only source of information, and some of the most traditionally minded among them still revere the written word above all else. By the late twentieth century, however, many professional historians had come to accept—partly through their forays into anthropology—that nonwritten (or "nontraditional") sources can also provide valuable insights into the past. Today's historians, like today's archaeologists, regularly examine a host of sources, including the following:

- Documents written by eyewitnesses
- Official records, such as deeds, legal petitions, and governmental regulations
- Newspaper stories
- Ethnographic accounts
- Folklore and folklife studies
- Recorded oral accounts of living men and women
- Transcriptions of oral accounts collected in the past
- Archaeologists' site reports
- Standing buildings and structures
- Photographs
- Maps, plans, and charts

The perspective that history can be told from a diverse collection of material has significantly broadened the conception of what constitutes a historical "source." Some historians have even acknowledged the importance of material culture as useful sources. For example, in *From Reliable*

Sources, historians Martha Howell and Walter Prevenier define sources in a broad way that includes artifacts: "[sources are] those materials from which historians construct meanings. Put another way, a source is an object from the past or testimony concerning the past on which historians depend in order to create their own depiction of that past." This definition indicates two important things about how many of today's historians think. First, it shows they consider archaeologically collected artifacts as legitimate historical sources (because artifacts come from "the past"), and, second, they have no difficulty seeing archaeologists as their colleagues in the study of history.

In chapter 3, we learned that archaeologists (and historians) write chronicles (Howell and Prevenier's "depictions") from the facts they have selected from their amassed sources. But an important question to ask is, Are all sources alike? Does every source have equal merit as evidence?

Historians recognize two general kinds of sources: primary and secondary. The difference between the two is extremely significant because the way in which a person selects his or her sources can help determine whether he or she is a true authority on a particular subject (see chapter 4). So how do primary and secondary sources differ?

In *The Future of History*, historian John Lukacs writes that primary sources are all those that "have been written or spoken by the subject of research." He describes secondary sources as accounts "of acts or words reported or recorded by someone else." Using these definitions, we can say that an archaeological excavation produces primary sources (artifacts and other remains) and that archaeologists use these to create their depictions of the past. These depictions, or chronicles, constitute secondary sources. Rather than being "written or spoken" as Lukacs would have it, the archaeologically collected artifacts are fashioned, purchased, used, and discarded by the subjects of research.

Some historical works can be difficult to define as primary or secondary. The writings of Herodotus and Thucydides fall into this category. Their fifth-century BCE histories are primary sources because each one witnessed and wrote about what they saw happening around them. Their writings are very old sources of information about the ancient world, but they are also secondary sources because their histories are depictions of the past as they interpreted it. Archaeologists frequently employ their texts as primary sources even though they are technically also secondary sources.

Archaeologically collected materials are also ambiguous but in a different way. Artifacts removed from the earth were clearly made and used in the past; they are primary sources that archaeologists use to interpret or "depict" history. Archaeological site reports are secondary sources because they present the archaeologist's depiction of the past. But these same secondary sources may also serve as primary-source materials if the archaeologist has included within them accurate artifact counts, measurements, scale drawings, and photographs. Since the reports contain primary data, other archaeologists can use these secondary sources as if they are primary sources. Site reports represent an archaeologist's interaction with the archaeological deposits in a manner that is similar to an eyewitness account of a historical event.

Archaeologists also produce pure secondary sources. Besides site reports and scholarly articles, some archaeologists write nontechnical, popular accounts by relying on primary archaeological sources. Brian Fagan's *The Great Journey*, mentioned in chapter 4, constitutes a secondary source because he presents a depiction of the peopling of North America using the research of other archaeologists (as primary sources). Science writers' best-selling books also fall into this category. Rather than conducting the research themselves, they take the works of other scholars and condense them in ways that tell compelling scientific accounts.

Every archaeologist, regardless of area of expertise, should be familiar with the evaluation of primary sources. The need for personal familiarity with the most relevant sources is one reason that archaeologists often visit museums and universities to study existing artifact collections. Every researcher must verify what the original archaeologists have included in their site reports to determine whether anything new can be learned from old collections. Ideas change and methods improve with the introduction of new concepts and the development of innovative technologies, and the study of existing artifact collections—containing primary-source artifacts—can advance knowledge. At the same time, scholars working with primary materials (documents and artifacts) realize that strong connections exist between the past and the present, a topic that historian Carl Becker explored in the early twentieth century (see chapter 3). Renowned French historian Fernand Braudel put the situation succinctly when he observed, "Past and present illuminate each other reciprocally." Each of us evaluates the past in terms of the present. Historians have taught archaeologists that no substitute exists for the personal examination of primary-source materials, and good archaeo-thinkers must learn to interpret primary sources. After all, letters, diaries, maps, charts, sketches, photographs, interview transcriptions, and legal documents are artifacts, too. (Years ago, one researcher suggested the term "manufacts" for manuscripts to indicate that they are really artifacts. Thankfully, however, the term never caught on!)

One reason that historians are so dedicated to the examination of primary sources is because they realize that only through direct contact with such materials can they provide new interpretations. A flash of insight may come from reading a secondary source—and this is wonderful when it happens—but no substitute exists for having a historical document directly in front of you. A case from my own experience offers a useful example.

While excavating a plantation site in rural South Carolina in the early 1980s, I wanted to know when the last residents finally moved away from the property. This information would have a direct bearing on how we understood the history of the property once all the residents had moved away. One of the truths of archaeology is that every human settlement—wherever it is in the world—continues to be influenced by human, animal, biological, and climatic activity long after its residents have abandoned it. This realization had consequences for my research because one of my main goals was to understand the changes that had occurred in the community after 1865, once the institution of slavery had been dismantled and the en-slaved had become tenant farmers. When I first saw the plantation site in 1981, all that remained were partly buried stone foundations. No buildings stood anywhere on the densely wooded property.

I knew from primary sources that a man named James Edward Cal-houn had owned and developed the plantation in 1834 but that the Afri-can American residents—originally held there in bondage—continued to live on the site until about 1925 even though Calhoun had died in 1889. Sometime after 1925, the residents had either died or moved away. One of the archaeological mysteries, then, was how long their houses and other buildings had remained standing. Nearby residents had revealed that in the 1920s, many people had begun to use the old plantation grounds as a picnic and camping spot. The site was located on the picturesque Savannah River, so its use for recreation made sense. I was unable to verify, how-ever, whether the local residents' memories were primary sources (they had actually seen campers on the property or been campers themselves) or secondary sources (they had been told about camping by someone else). It dawned on me that people on such outings often take pictures and that these images, if they exist, might show the presence of standing buildings at the site. A search of photographs kept by local residents in scrapbooks or in their attics yielded one or two faded pictures that substantiated the veracity of the oral testimony; people had indeed used the site for outings after about 1925. One or two of these old photos even showed some of the old buildings in their backgrounds, indicating that some had remained standing until the early 1950s. These photographic documents filled an important gap in our knowledge about the history of the plantation. When we excavated at the site, the discovery of post-1925 bottles, cans, and other objects provided further support for the history of the place after it had long ceased operation as a plantation.

Many archaeologists undoubtedly have similar experiences. How many pictures do you think, for example, have been taken by people visiting Stonehenge, Cahokia Mounds, and the Parthenon over the years? If compiled into a single repository and analyzed, what might they depict with archaeological significance? Would they show the rate of decay, incidences of vandalism, and the variety of activities that have occurred at these ancient places long after the original builders had disappeared?

The careful study of primary sources of whatever sort can provide startling new interpretations of history. An especially fascinating example comes from the Declaration of Independence, a document many may feel they already know quite well.

Reading the Declaration of Independence

If you visit the U.S. Capitol Rotunda, you can stand before a massive painting titled *The Declaration of Independence*. Measuring 12 by 18 feet (3.6 by 5.5 meters), this painting by John Trumbull depicts the signing of the declaration by the assembled members of the Continental Congress. The image is so famous that you may actually be able to picture it in your mind. John Adams, Thomas Jefferson, and Benjamin Franklin stand prominently in front of a table, handing the declaration to the seated John Hancock, the president of the Congress. The delegates, all men, sit or stand contemplatively in the left background, eyewitnesses to history. Even though Trumbull completed the painting in 1818—a full 46 years after the event—it remains an iconic image of the founding of the United States. In fact, the image appears on the back of a $2 bill. The only problem with this picture is that it's not true. The event Trumbull portrayed never happened. This startling history could be proven only by the study of primary sources.

In *After the Fact*, their book on historical methods, historians James Davidson and Mark Lytle observe that when historians began to examine the primary sources about the signing of the declaration, they discovered three surprising things:

1. The Continental Congress declared independence from Great Britain on July 2, not on July 4.
2. Most of the members of the Congress signed the document on August 2, not on July 4.
3. All of the signers never met in the same place to sign the document.

An equally surprising finding—and one that destroys what most Americans have been taught—is that Thomas Jefferson was not the document's sole author. In truth, many people can claim a piece of the authorship because several delegates added their own ideas to what would become the final text.

The members of the Continental Congress who were charged with preparing the proclamation of independence encouraged Jefferson to prepare the draft, which he promptly did. (Actually, the evidence indicates he wrote several drafts.) After completing the draft to his satisfaction, he sent it to Franklin and Adams, both of whom added their own comments and alterations in the margins. Jefferson took these suggestions to heart, made a new copy of the declaration (with their comments included), and then sent the revised draft to Congress. This text circulated to the delegates, and each man (they were all men) was free to add his own suggestions. Before they were finished, the delegates had removed about one-quarter of Jefferson's original text.

All of this was unknown after the deaths of the delegates. It was not until 1947 that an enterprising historian discovered the drafts that revealed the true history of the declaration. The document's history is written directly on the drafts themselves. They show that delegates had crossed out and changed phrases, added words above sentences, and interjected entirely new paragraphs. In all, they made 86 changes to Jefferson's draft (figure 6.1). The beautifully scripted document you see on display at the National Archives—behind several inches of thick glass—is not the copy with which most delegates were familiar.

The story of the Declaration of Independence shows that no substitute exists for the personal examination of primary sources. Historians rely on primary-source examination as their bread and butter, and the well-trained archaeo-thinker must appreciate the value of learning from their experience.

In their study of the Declaration of Independence, Davidson and Lytle present tactics to help historians understand documents. Three of their tactics are relevant to archaeological research:

1. *First read the document to get an understanding of its general content.* What this somewhat self-evident tactic means is that a document must be thoroughly read before its deep meanings can be comprehended. This reading provides a basic understanding of what the author was attempting to get across and how he or she perceived what was most important. For example, the writers of the Declaration of Independence stressed their central, unmistakable point right in the

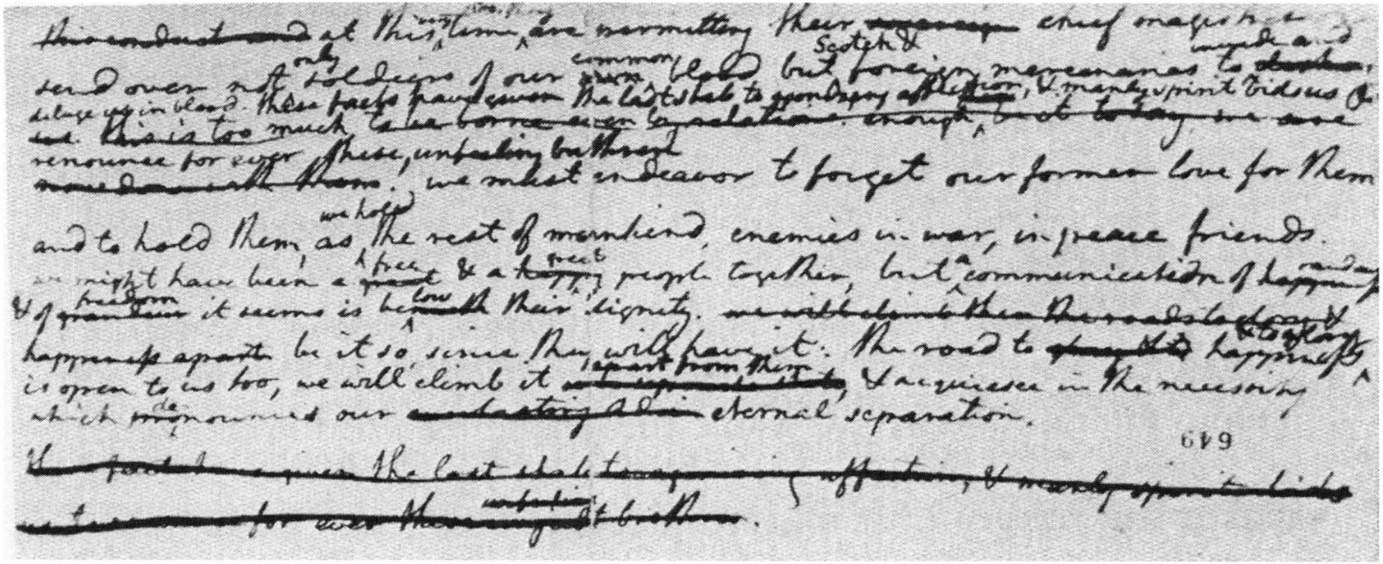

Figure 6.1. Edits on the Declaration of Independence. Library of Congress.

title: "The unanimous declaration of the thirteen united states of America." They unambiguously stated from the start that they were 1) unanimous, and (2) they represented 13 "united states," not 13 Crown colonies. For archaeologists, an initial reading may involve the typical primary sources (letters, diaries, travel accounts, and so forth), but it may also involve reading another archaeologist's field notes, plan drawings, site maps, and excavation records. This first reading will provide an understanding of the documents' contents and create a feel for the subject matter.

2. *Establish the context of the document and question what was left out.* Davidson and Lytle note that Jefferson wanted to include in the Declaration of Independence a statement of how the English monarchy had violated basic human rights by promoting African slavery. But the slave-owning delegates, demanding that this statement not appear in the final draft, got their way, and nothing about slavery was mentioned. The Declaration's silence on one of the darkest aspects of American history thus represents a huge void in the document.

   For archaeologists, the context of site-related documents may include studying what another archaeologist decided to ignore in his or her field notes. For example, an archaeologist concerned with environment reconstruction might be inclined, perhaps unconsciously, to spend less time documenting the spatial distribution of pottery sherds discovered during an excavation. His or her notes may contain detailed information about the distribution of seeds and other plant materials but little else. Another archaeologist might not notice the seeds at all. Other archaeologists, interested only in ancient history, may ignore the more recently dated artifacts at a site. In each case, what is missing is important.

3. *Seek to reconstruct the intellectual world in existence at the time a document was created.* When the United States was founded, the tenets of the Enlightenment held sway within the educated upper class, a group including the delegates of the Continental Congress. Jefferson and his colleagues were conversant with the leading European Enlightenment scholars and their works. Some of them even knew the prominent intellectuals personally. The Declaration of Independence presents all the Enlightenment's central values: a commitment to freedom of conscience, liberty, and free expression. That the delegates could so easily ignore slavery shows the historical context of language. When the delegates wrote about "freedom,"

they referred only to their fellow class members rather than to the "lower orders" and certainly not to the millions of men, women, and children of African descent who lived throughout the 13 new states. The delegates' eighteenth-century concept of "freedom" is much different from its twenty-first-century meaning.

For archaeologists, understanding the intellectual atmosphere of an era involves knowing something about the theoretical trends within the discipline. Much of the research in the social sciences, including anthropological archaeology, takes its lead from what is occurring in society at large. In the 1960s, archaeologists became serious about environmental reconstruction in concert with the rise of the ecology movement, and the growth in ethnic awareness encouraged historical archaeologists to study New World enslavement. The feminist movement has had a tremendous impact on archaeological research, as has recent thinking about the relationships between human rights and archaeological heritage. The fall of the Berlin Wall compelled some archaeologists to conduct investigations into the architecture of the Cold War, leading to the documentation of missile silos and bomb shelters. Future archaeologists will undoubtedly turn their attention toward global warming and the historical challenges of water acquisition.

Once the social context of archaeology is understood, we can begin to see that it, like all cultural, social, and historical analysis, is not detached from the present. Archaeologists live in the same world as everyone else, and they are profoundly affected by what goes on around them. The same was true of Jefferson, Adams, and Franklin.

The men who wrote the Declaration of Independence did so when it was relevant to them. The document belongs very much to their time. The authors wrote, rewrote, and finalized it in 1776; they announced it in 1776; and citizens and politicians felt its impact in 1776. This document will be forever associated with that date. In fact, one of the problems faced by policymakers in twenty-first-century America is to devise ways to make laws consistent with the ideals expressed in the late eighteenth-century document.

Even though 1776 seems like a long time ago, it is a relatively recent time in the broad sweep of human history. But even in the course of this relatively short time span, the history that people thought they knew about one of the era's most important documents was dramatically altered by examining primary documents. If we can be surprised by a document that is so well known and not terribly old, what does this say about older documents and accounts written by writers who lived generations before Jefferson and Franklin, writers whom Jefferson and Franklin, as eighteenth-century scholars, would have found interesting themselves? This question is pertinent to archaeo-thinking because archaeologists must often rely on very old manuscripts.

Time matters. A significant gap in time between witnessing an event and writing down an account of it can be crucial in helping scholars assess the reliability of a historical document. A time gap between an ethnographic observation and an archaeological expression is equally meaningful. Binford's ethnographic analogy was weakened by the gap between the occupation dates of the Toothsome Site and the dates of his various eyewitness accounts (see chapter 5).

Because archaeologists may confront temporal gaps when they consult historical sources, archaeo-thinkers must appreciate the impact such gaps can have on interpretation. The rule of thumb is that *the shorter the gap between the event and its transcription, the more likely is the transcription to be accurate (unless the author has purposefully been dishonest)*. An ancient tale with a significant archaeological component demonstrates the problem represented by a large gap between event and document.

The Search for Saint Brendan the Navigator

One of the enduring mysteries of world history is the question of who, if anyone, from the Old World discovered America before Columbus. Archaeology, because of its unique ability to discover hard evidence in the earth, is especially well suited to addressing this question. In fact, archaeologists did answer it, at least partially, in the 1960s when they discovered a medieval Norse settlement at L'Anse aux Meadows in today's Newfoundland. The Vikings had beaten Columbus to the New World by almost 500 years. Since then, many have continued to wonder whether anyone else could have made the transatlantic voyage before them. Popular choices for pre-Viking visitors to the New World include the Lost Tribes of Israel, the medieval Welsh, and West Africans. A perennial favorite has been medieval Irish monks under the leadership of Saint Brendan.

Believers in the Saint Brendan claim say that sixth-century CE Irish monks made landfall somewhere in northeastern North America, building heavy stone structures wherever they went. The believers support their claim by citing the presence of solidly built stone structures in New England. Many of these structures bear a remarkable resemblance to ancient stone-built passage tombs in Ireland. But are they related?

The true believers' faith in the early Irish presence in North America rests entirely on old manuscripts referring to Saint Brendan's voyage. The fullest account of his trip is the *Navigatio Sancti Brendani Abbatis* (*The Voyage of Saint Brendan the Abbot*). An analysis of this primary document sheds light on the likelihood that Brendan reached North America, or what the manuscript calls "The Land Promised to the Saints." But is the *Navigatio* a reliable source for archaeologists to take seriously?

Saint Brendan was a real Irish monk who lived from about 489 to 570 or 583 CE. He is almost as famous in Ireland as Saint Patrick. Whereas Saint Patrick is renowned for bringing Christianity to pagan Ireland— and for chasing away the island's snakes (an archaeologist's dream come true!)—Saint Brendan is revered for his supposed voyage to North America hundreds of years before Columbus. He is the patron saint of seafarers, and writers often refer to him as Saint Brendan "the Navigator" to commemorate his alleged transatlantic journey.

Scholars have had difficulty dating it, but the *Navigatio* contains the most complete account of Brendan's voyage. If Brendan and his crew of fellow monks made the trip, it logically had to have been during his lifetime, or between 489 and 570–583. The very earliest date that medieval scholars can assign to the *Navigatio* is 800, and some of the manuscripts (there are at least 120 of various lengths) date to the 900s and even later. If we accept that the document's earliest date is 800, the gap between the voyage and the document is either 217 (from 583 CE) or 230 years (from 570 CE). To put this into perspective, this is equivalent to writing down an account today of something that occurred just after the American War of Independence. The time gap is tremendous, but it does not necessarily disqualify the *Navigatio* as a legitimate source. Oral tradition may have kept it alive for years. Perhaps someone finally decided to commit to parchment a story that everyone already knew quite well.

Oral tradition is a valuable source of information. After collaborating with numerous indigenous groups around the world, archaeologists have verified that long-held traditions and stories can be reliable sources of historical and cultural information. People in many cultures have a remarkable ability to remember and pass on their traditions in spoken form. Even so, the good archaeological thinker cannot afford to regard oral information uncritically, any more than the written word can be accepted at face value.

With oral information, we must be aware of the "telephone effect." The name comes from the game you may have played as a child. Everyone sits in a circle and whispers a story to one another in succession. The effect is that the story changes slightly with each retelling. If this can happen in a brief, silly game, what is the effect of hundreds of years of retelling? The passage of time does not invalidate oral tradition, but it does necessitate caution when using it.

We can employ the tactics mentioned by Davidson and Lytle to delve into the *Navigatio*. The first tactic is simply to read it.

One of the first things you learn when reading the *Navigatio* is that Brendan and his crew did not leave the coast of western Ireland, sail in a straight line, and arrive at the Land Promised to the Saints seven years later. Actually, he and his crew zigzagged across the Atlantic, first heading west, then east, then west again. Knowing that the voyage was haphazard weakens the view that Brendan was a great navigator. On the contrary, his crew sometimes stopped rowing their curragh (the name for a small, skin-covered boat used in Ireland), stowed its sail, and simply allowed God to take them wherever He wanted them to go. Reading the *Navigatio* gives the impression that the voyage was completely unscripted, that the crew simply wandered around in the Atlantic until they spotted an island to land on. Brendan actually had to do little true navigating.

Another important understanding emerging from the *Navigatio* is that it does not read as a travelogue. It reads like a religious text presenting a Christian message rather than a geographically accurate ship's log.

The *Navigatio* belongs to a body of religious medieval literature, and, as a result, scholars have had trouble separating its truth from its allegory. Medieval Christian writers usually filled their works with allegorical and symbolic meanings intended to impress their readers and listeners. At a time when many people were illiterate and books were scarce, priests could relate the central messages of Christianity with well-known phrases and images. For instance, the author of the *Navigatio* mentions the number "3" repeatedly. Brendan and his crew stay in one place for three days, they sail for three days, they meet three choirs, and so on. In one spot, the text reads, "When, then, they had circled the island for *three* days, on the *third* day about *three* o'clock they found an opening where one boat might enter." Medieval Christians placed great emphasis on the number three because of its association with the Holy Trinity, and its frequent mention in the *Navigatio* cannot be accidental. The number "7" is another powerful numerical symbol for Christians. It appears many times in the Bible, most prominently to refer to the creation of the Earth and the day on which God rested. The text also uses "40 days" to mean "a long time." This number represents another important symbol for Christians. It refers to the duration of the rain causing the Great Flood (40 days and 40 nights) and to the time Moses spent on the mount awaiting the Ten Commandments.

Thus, when the *Navigatio* mentions "40 days" of sailing, it doesn't mean 40 actual calendar days; it simply means "a long time."

Some of the stories in the *Navigatio* are clearly fantastic. In line with much of the pre-Columbian exploration literature, the *Navagatio* relates that Brendan and his crew encountered many strange creatures. On one tiny island, for instance, a dog led them to a settlement with a formal hall containing a linen-covered table laid with a full meal. Brendan's crew never saw a single person during their three-day (!) stay on the island, but the food was always prepared and ready. On another island, they encountered three (!) choirs, one dressed all in white, one all in blue, and the third all in purple. On another island, they met tiny black demons, which, in the translation I used, are referred to as "Ethiopians." On another island, they met and conversed with Judas, who told Brendan that he had "purchased" his cruel fate with "an evil bargain." My favorite example by far is the story of Jasconius the whale.

The monks first encountered Jasconius on Easter Sunday. Thinking the animal was a smooth, treeless island, the monks beached their boat on its back. When they started a fire, however, the "island" began to shake. The monks, in fear for their lives, quickly scrambled back into their tiny boat, where the ever-wise Brendan had remained. Brendan explained to his terrified crew that the "island" was simply a "fish"—indeed, the largest fish in the sea but a fish nonetheless. For the next seven years, Brendan and his crew celebrated every Easter on the back of Jasconius. Many medieval illustrators, apparently never having seen a whale, depicted it as a giant fish (figure 6.2).

The context of the document is perfectly consistent with the medieval religious world, a time when monks made pilgrimages, established monasteries in pagan regions, and transcribed manuscripts. The goal of Brendan's crews is in keeping with much medieval literature.

One of the goals of modern researchers who believe the Brendan story is to identify real places with those mentioned in the *Navigatio*. For example, they identify North America as the "Land Promised to the Saints." Knowing Brendan's final destination, we can ask a simple question: how many stories do you know ending with a brave hero overcoming all odds to reach a Promised Land?

Some of the places mentioned in the *Navigatio* can be identified as real. These include the Faroe Islands, Iceland, and the Shetland Islands. A general consensus among scholars is that the Island of Sheep and the Paradise of Birds are the Faroe Islands; the Island of Smiths was most likely southern Iceland, and the Fiery Mountain may have been Hekla, one of

Den schwanz regete so wond der qual von dem wasser als groß
vor dem schiff das er den kiel off hub als ober

ir die lufft wolte tragen vnd viel den wider her nider
als ob er yn abgrund wolte wasser dem selben fisch was
das vff den schmaltz gewachsen holtz vnd graß do wachssid so alle

Figure 6.2.   Medieval German image of Saint Brendan and his crew on the back of Jasconius the Whale. From *Manusriptum translationis germanicae*, Cod. Pal. Germ. 60, fol. 179v. Courtesy the Heidelberg University Library, Germany.

Iceland's most active volcanoes. The Column of Crystal was undoubtedly an iceberg, and Jasconius the "fish" was obviously a whale.

But what some readers find most intriguing are references to places that bear no relationship to these identifiable places. These references—to water so clear that the monks can see all the way to the bottom, bushes full of grapes, and trees with strange fruit—are what keeps alive the idea that Brendan discovered America. The central question, then, is, Are these references enough to make the story of Brendan's discovery of America believable or at least plausible?

Seeking to answer this question, adventurer Tim Severin planned a trip across the Atlantic in a replica of a skin-covered curragh, much like the one Brendan may have used. He read works by scholars (secondary sources) who had pored over the various manuscripts (primary sources) seeking to correlate real places with the islands mentioned in the various texts. Severin assumed that Brendan took a route from western Ireland to Iceland and then on to Newfoundland and possibly even to the clear, warm waters of the Caribbean. Severin's voyage lasted from May 1976 to June 1977. He actually did make it to Newfoundland, but he went no farther. His voyage proved that the trip was possible in the late 1970s, but was it possible hundreds of years earlier? And what about the Caribbean and the clear water the monks saw?

In keeping with Davidson and Lytle's tactics, we can ask, What's missing from the *Navigatio*? One of the most telling aspects of the text is that Brendan never meets anyone who would be unfamiliar to a medieval reader or listener. He meets singing choirs, Judas, a community of silent monks, Paul the Hermit, and people who always seem able to feed the crew, just as medieval monks in Europe assisted passing pilgrims. Missing is any reference to contacts with or even any sightings of the New World's native peoples. Cultural historian Geoffrey Ashe, in *Land to the West*, identifies the little "black demons" (the "Ethiopians") as Eskimos, noting that Viking texts often described them in these terms. But, in keeping with the religious intent of the *Navigatio*, these demons are portrayed as otherworldly and spiritually dangerous rather than as culturally unfamiliar. Failure to mention non-Europeans is revealing. Columbus noted in his journal that when landing on what he named San Salvador, which the Indians called Guanahani, he immediately saw "naked people." The native islanders did not shy away from Columbus on their first encounter. So why didn't Brendan see any indigenous peoples? It remains quite possible that no one may have been around when Brendan visited the West Indies. It seems logical to conclude, though, that even a brief mention of "strange non-believers" would be fodder for a religious tract such as the *Navigatio*.

It appears noteworthy as well that the *Navigatio* makes no mention of any unfamiliar pieces of material culture, nor does it at any time state that Brendan built structures (of any kind) anywhere he went. The crew did encounter already existing and completely recognizable structures, such as the Community of Ailbe's monastery (on an island that, by the way, they had to circle for 40 days before they could find a landing spot). Absolutely no mention is made of any construction by Brendan's crew and certainly not on the islands reputed to be the New World. Constructing stone buildings would have been major events that would have taken the monks many days to complete. The *Navigatio*'s failure to mention them represents a huge hole that true believers cannot close with wishful thinking.

Archaeology, coupled with known texts, proves that Irish monks did reach the relatively nearby northern isles of Scotland, the Faroes, and Iceland in the eighth century. Scholars have been able to attach these places with islands mentioned in the *Navigatio* with some measure of certainty. Linking the voyage to the West Indies and New England is considerably less believable. The context of the *Navigatio* as a religious tract, the numerous motifs that appear in it and other religious texts, and the lack of archaeological evidence anywhere in the New World make the case for Brendan's discovery of America extremely weak. Because Severin was able to reach North America in the mid-1970s, it remains *possible* that Brendan and his crew may have reached North America in the sixth century, but the careful archaeo-thinker must remain highly skeptical of the claim until concrete evidence is unearthed.

One question worth asking is, How could true believers of the voyage accept some parts of the *Navigatio* as true (the identifiable islands in the North Atlantic) and ignore the allegory (the more religious-sounding parts)? Why should they suppose that the author (or authors) of the *Navigatio* was only being truthful as a geographer? The answer lies in the mistake of discovering what one hopes to find rather than allowing the evidence to be the guide. The *Navigatio Sancti Brendani Abbatis* is a poor archaeological primary source even though fringe scholars and true believers in "secret, hidden history" continue to promote the notion that Brendan's crew built ancient Celtic structures in North America.

The attachment of New England's stone structures to the Brendan story introduces a tangible archaeological element. Without linking these buildings to the *Navigatio*, true believers in Brendan's discovery of America can only extrapolate using a rather typical religious tract from the Middle

Ages. The addition of stone structures provides believers with a sense of truth even though the *Navigatio* never mentions (or even implies) that Brendan's crew raised buildings anywhere they landed. Nonetheless, stone buildings in New England—which can be visited, experienced, and even touched today—imbue the story with a degree of concreteness for those who wish to believe in Saint Brendan.

People untrained in archaeology make the mistake of associating cultural features from one culture with those of another culture simply because they may look alike. Good archaeo-thinkers appreciate that many perfectly reasonable explanations for similarity between structures may exist without calling on an ancient culture located thousands of miles away. Connecting the Celts with North America in this manner merely represents the construction of a poor analogy. Is it more likely that ancient Irish monks came to North America and for some reason constructed elaborate stone structures (leaving no other trace), or is it more plausible that eighteenth-century Irish immigrants, familiar with the ancient structures at home, mimicked them in the New World and used them as root cellars? Cool, dark places are excellent for storing farm produce before the invention of refrigeration, and stone-built cellars would provide a perfect environment. Every time professional archaeologists excavate one of these stone structures in New England, they only find Native American and European colonial artifacts. No one has ever found any legitimate ancient Celtic artifacts in North America. All of the evidence indicates that the structures were colonial-era root cellars or special-use buildings and that medieval Irish monks had nothing to do with them.

Archaeologists understand that just like written sources, material objects demand careful and thoughtful interpretation. In the next chapter, then, we turn to ways that good archaeological thinkers can understand artifacts.

Continue Reading

Saint Brendan

Ashe, Geoffrey. 1962. *Land to the West: St. Brendan's Voyage to America.* New York: Viking Press.

Markham, Clements R., ed. 1893. *The Journal of Christopher Columbus (during His First Voyage, 1492–93) and Documents Relating to the Voyages of John Cabot and Gaspar Corte Real.* London: Hakluyt Society.

O'Meara, John J. 1991. *The Voyage of Saint Brendan: Journey to the Promised Land.* Gerrards Cross: Colin Smythe.

Severin, Tim. 2000. *The Brendan Voyage.* New York: Modern Library.

Waddell, Helen, ed. 1952. *Mediaeval Latin Lyrics.* Baltimore: Penguin.

Source-Thinking

Braudel, Fernand. 1980. *On History*. Translated by Sarah Matthews. Chicago: University of Chicago Press.

Davidson, James West, and Mark Hamilton Lytle. 2009. *After the Fact: The Art of Historical Detection*. 6th ed. New York: McGraw-Hill.

Deetz, James. 1967. *Invitation to Archaeology*. Garden City, NY: Natural History Press.

Fischer, David Hackett. 1970. *Historian's Fallacies: Toward a Logic of Historical Thought*. New York: Harper and Row.

Howell, Martha, and Walter Prevenier. 2001. *From Reliable Sources: An Introduction to Historical Methods*. Ithaca, NY: Cornell University Press.

Lukacs, John. 2011. *The Future of History*. New Haven, CT: Yale University Press.

Orser, Charles E., Jr. 2013. The Politics of Periodization. In *Reclaiming Archaeology: Beyond the Tropes of Modernity*, edited by Alfredo González-Ruibal, 145–54. London: Routledge.

Wolf, Eric R. 1982. *Europe and the People without History*. Berkeley: University of California Press.

Artifact-Thinking
Archaeological Thought and
Excavated Things

7

ONE THING EVERYONE SEEMS TO KNOW about archaeology—except perhaps people who think archaeologists study dinosaurs—is that the field involves artifacts. The popularity of the Indiana Jones movies helped to instill the idea that archaeologists slash through jungles and prowl through caves searching for golden idols, precious works of ancient art, and magical charms. This swashbuckling image is true to some extent. Many archaeologists conduct fieldwork in exotic, dangerous places and occasionally find one-of-a-kind works of art. (Though today's archaeologists do much more record keeping than the fictional Dr. Jones!) Excavated golden statues, painted clay pots, and jade bracelets are just the things museum curators love to exhibit as soon as they acquire them. The greatest discoveries make the news worldwide. Editors, television producers, and museum curators all recognize the general public's fascination with history's beautiful, unique objects.

In reality, archaeologists rarely find a museum piece that attracts international attention. They are much more likely to unearth mundane things people used every day in their homes, religious centers, and backyards. In his wickedly funny *Bluff Your Way in Archaeology*, Paul Bahn observes that "if history is bunk, then archaeology is junk." He isn't too far off the mark. In fact, openly accepting the archaeologist's interest in junk led archaeologist William Rathje to invent a subfield called "garbology." Garbologists like Rathje use archaeological methods, insights, and perspectives to analyze present-day trash dumps and landfills. Like all archaeologists, they know that stories of daily life lie hidden within the objects people used, discarded, and lost throughout their lifetimes. Everyday objects are the fragments archaeologists use to reveal the realities of the past.

Archaeologists collect a great deal of information besides artifacts, but the analysis of physical remains is the bread and butter of archaeological research. The interest that archaeologists have in artifacts is what makes their discipline unique. As archaeologist Michael Schiffer has stated, "Whether their interests are in prehistoric, historical, industrial, classical, or modern societies, archaeologists are preoccupied with discerning how people and artifacts interact." The physical objects capturing the archaeologist's attention range from the smallest flint chip to the largest industrial buildings and rural landscapes.

The daunting task that archaeologists face when trying to unravel an artifact's past meaning can be grasped by thinking about the millions of things individuals have used since human history began. Museums are filled to overflowing with historical artifacts, and what visitors usually see on display is a tiny percentage of what most institutions hold in storage.

Given the immense variety of the objects archaeologists may potentially find and study, no one should be surprised that individual archaeologists may interpret artifacts in distinctly different ways. Some archaeologists may emphasize how artifacts help people survive in their environments, and others may view artifacts as symbolic representations of a cultural practice or idea. Some archaeologists may adopt several perspectives throughout their careers as their ideas change and their knowledge grows. This process is a normal part of archaeological research.

When choosing to adopt one perspective over others, archaeologists must adhere to the principles presented in the earlier chapters. Archaeological interpretations must be based on logic and specific knowledge of the historical and cultural contexts of the people and place under study. The interpretations must be as plausible as the state of knowledge will permit. Pseudo-archaeologists' ideas fail simply because they violate the rules of sound archaeological reasoning. Pure speculation, based on imagination rather than cultural and historical reality, has no place in serious archaeological scholarship.

Before delving into some of the issues surrounding artifacts, an additional point is worth mentioning. The previous chapter presented some similarities between artifacts and written records and observed that archaeologists approach both as pieces of material culture. A white and blue teacup fragment presents the same challenges of analysis and interpretation as a letter written in 1732. Even so, the two objects are not similar. Excavated artifacts and archived written records have at least one significant difference.

Textual records of whatever sort—letters, diaries, governmental papers, inscriptions, and so forth—represent someone's conscious effort to make their thoughts permanent. The documents' authors expected others to read what they had memorialized on paper. Artifacts, on the other hand, may not necessarily be intended to be permanent in the same way. Archaeologist Katherine Howlett Hayes draws an insightful distinction between written records and archaeologically discovered artifacts. She observes that extant written records are objects that have been *selected*, meaning that an individual sat down and committed his or her thoughts to paper. From that time forward, someone else has seen fit to preserve the document in a personal collection, archive, or library. Without this process of conscious selection, no one alive today would know about the document.

Artifacts found in the earth by archaeologists tend to be objects *not selected* for preservation until they are discovered. Once aboveground, the archaeologist or museum curator will preserve and protect the artifacts just as an archivist would an important document. The central point, though, is that individuals who discarded artifacts—a broken spear point, a cracked bottle, or a half button—did not expect or intend for anyone to discover them. In some cases, people may have thrown away objects specifically in the hope that no one would ever find them. During the prohibition era in the United States (1920–1933), whiskey bottles tossed down a family's well would be an apt example!

When confronted with a collection of artifacts, archaeologists must decide how to interpret them. (Here we leave aside the myriad other archaeological evidence and concentrate specifically on the artifacts themselves as if they exist in isolation, which they most certainly do not.) If we assume that all professionally trained archaeologists are equally adept at properly identifying artifacts, the major question is then, How do archaeologists make sense of them? How do archaeologists decide what artifacts *mean* within the social, cultural, and historical contexts in which the objects were once situated?

Resolving this question is the archaeologist's most difficult challenge. The different ways individual archaeologists have sought to think to some purpose about artifacts have provided the fuel for creating different points of view in the discipline. Disagreements between the various theoretical camps have caused controversy. The conflicts have significantly advanced archaeological knowledge, however, because individual archaeologists have been encouraged to consider alternate ideas and ponder new perspectives.

The goal of this chapter is not to guide you through the maze of ideas or to argue for any particular mode of analysis or theoretical perspective—that will come as you continue your archaeological studies. My purpose is to present three ways archeologists can interpret artifacts. Like our ancestors, all of us surround ourselves every day with a variety of things.

Understanding the past relationships with these objects is a key feature of archaeological thinking.

Three prominent ways archaeologists have thought about artifacts has been as historical documents (what they reveal about the history of the times, including providing information about dates), as commodities (what they say about cultural interaction and exchanges), and as ideas (what complex concepts artifacts may communicate). Objects familiar to everyone—white-bodied ceramic dishes—provide a useful example.

Ceramics as Historical Documents

All archaeologists accept the basic assumption that artifacts provide information about the past. The most basic feature of any artifact is its date. Archaeologists wish to understand, first and foremost, the age of an artifact so they know where to place it along the scale of human history. Archaeologists provide dates for artifacts in numerous ways, extending from the stylistic attributes of the artifacts themselves to sophisticated, high-tech testing of their chemical properties. Archaeologists typically date the ceramics from the late eighteenth to early twentieth centuries—the target group here—using a combination of stylistic features, information appearing directly on individual pieces, and historical records (pattern books, production records, and other potters' notes).

Archaeologists excavating late eighteenth- to late nineteenth-century sites usually divide the white-bodied ceramics they find into three gross categories: creamware, pearlware, and whiteware. They usually identify these types using the following characteristics:

Creamware: a slight yellowish or greenish cast on the surface, with green puddling or pooling in the crevices around handles and in the foot ring (the bead of clay around the base)

Pearlware: a slight bluish cast, whiter than creamware, with blue pooling in the crevices

Whiteware: whiter than pearlware, no blue or green cast, and no pooling in the crevices

These types are associated with specific periods of history because they represent the evolution in the English ceramics industry (figure 7.1). Creamware, invented first, dates from about 1762 to about 1820. Pearlware followed, being produced from about 1775 to the 1840s, and whiteware came last (1813 to the present). Many of the dishes you know may be whiteware because this ware is still widely available today.

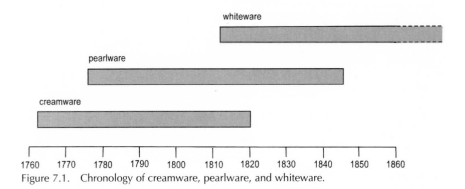

Figure 7.1.   Chronology of creamware, pearlware, and whiteware.

In addition to their physical properties, white-bodied ceramics can provide stylistic information. Like many artifacts, some styles were popular only for certain periods. (This is the battleship-shaped curve mentioned in chapter 1.) Beginning in the late eighteenth century and continuing up to today, ceramic producers decorated their vessels with a huge variety of colors, styles, and patterns. Archaeologists know that some styles can be dated with relative precision.

One wildly popular style in the nineteenth century was called shell-edged. This decorative style, usually applied to plates (but also applied to sugar bowls and other tablewares), is recognizable as a series of short, parallel, shallow scratches located along the rim (figure 7.2). On plates, the scratches extend around the entire rim, but on other vessels, potters put the decoration around the body of the vessel. Potters usually decorated the scratches with blue pigment, but sometimes they used green and even pink.

Over time and as styles changed, potters modified the shapes of the plate rims. From the beginning to the middle of the nineteenth century, shell-edged plates had scalloped rims, but during the late nineteenth century, the rims were left smooth. From about 1820 to about 1845, potters also put raised designs (such as feathers and floral motifs) on the rims in addition to the colored pigment (figure 7.3).

In addition to having stylistic attributes to signal date of manufacture, archaeologists know that many ceramic factories put their company names (and sometimes the name of the decorative pattern) directly on the bottom of their products. Before 1770, English ceramic producers seldom marked their pieces with their name, but after this date they almost always did so. Pattern marks were common in the mid-nineteenth century. Factories marked their wares because each one was in direct competition with the others, and individual manufacturers wanted their customers to be able to recognize their wares and patterns.

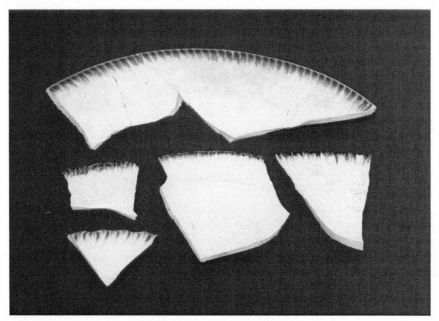

Figure 7.2.   Shell-edged pearlware. Photograph by Katherine L. Hull.

Potters often changed their bottom marks over time, and, given the usefulness of these "makers' marks" for dating and identification, ceramic specialists have compiled catalog books of them. Using these sources, archaeologists can determine that a bowl marked on the bottom with a globe having the word MINTON written across it was the product of the Minton ceramic works located in Staffordshire, England. This factory used the globe from about 1863 to 1872, but in 1873 it added a crown to the top of the globe and changed the word to MINTONS. An archaeologist unearthing a basal sherd with a globe and no crown could immediately

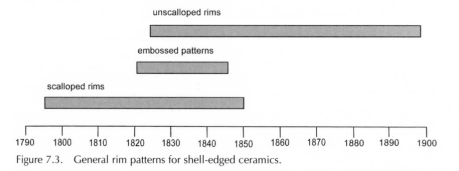

Figure 7.3.   General rim patterns for shell-edged ceramics.

date the piece to 1863–1872, whereas a piece with the crown included would date 1872–1912 (when the factory changed its bottom mark again). In addition to sometimes including makers' marks on their wares, British potters often included political messages. In 1765, during the Stamp Act crisis in the American colonies, British potters, seeking to entice American consumers, put pro-colony slogans on teapots, punch bowls, and other ceramic objects. Slogans like "No Stamp Act," "American Liberty Restored," "Stamp Act Repeal'd," and "Pitt and Liberty" were common. (William Pitt, a respected British statesman, had proclaimed the Stamp Act unconstitutional and was sympathetic to the idea of American liberty.) The discovery of these objects at a colonial-era archaeological site in the eastern United States would signal both a date (1765 or after) and a political sentiment (pro-American liberty).

In each case, the information that archaeologists can glean from ceramic artifacts functions to allow them to situate the artifacts in time and space. This research, based on excavated artifacts supplemented with written records, often provides information missing from textual sources. An archaeologist excavating a historically undocumented farmhouse in the American Midwest would immediately be able to date the house with the discovery of an earthenware sherd containing the Minton bottom mark (provided that the soil is undisturbed). The information from excavated artifacts can serve as unique and powerful historical documents collected from the archaeological archives located beneath the soil.

Ceramics as Commodities

The archaeologist excavating the farmhouse with the Minton sherd would immediately know that the bowl was not made in the United States. The bottom mark would reveal that the bowl was transported from Staffordshire, England, to its final resting place in the Midwest. Given that the Minton pottery factory was enmeshed in the modern market economy, the archaeologist would also know that the bowl once functioned as a commodity. A commodity is anything used specifically for exchange. The midwestern farmer had to trade a certain amount of money (pay the purchase price) with a merchant to obtain the Minton bowl. This is the same kind of economic transaction we practice today; we exchange one thing for another of equal economic value.

English factory owners transported their ceramic wares around the world, but they were not the first to have their wares shipped over vast distances. Chinese porcelain makers had begun the intercontinental sale of ceramics years earlier. In fact, English potters' desire to manufacture white-bodied wares was an effort to mimic Asian porcelain. Thus, the story of the English (and later American) ceramics industry is not confined to the British Isles. It has multicultural roots.

By the thirteenth century CE, China was poised to be the world's most powerful superpower because it had achieved a level of technological competence unmatched elsewhere. Part of the people's technical sophistication was expressed in their production of thin-bodied porcelain wares. These wares quickly became the envy of the world, a status they still enjoy today.

Chinese potters began producing intricately designed vessels during the Neolithic period (3000–1500 BCE), and they had made pots using potter's wheels by Han dynasty times (206 BCE–220 CE). By the ninth century CE, Islamic traders had expressed fascination with the quality of the pieces from Chinese kilns, and well before the thirteenth century, Chinese merchants participated in an international trade in porcelain. Chinese potters began the process of producing wares specifically for export, and their first, major trading partners were not Europeans.

Before the mid-sixteenth century, the principal non-Chinese consumers of porcelain lived in the Islamic world. Elite Muslims were so important to the porcelain industry that it may not have developed as it did without them. Europeans generated even greater demand when they arrived in Asia (the Portuguese in 1517 and the Dutch in 1601). The Ming dynasty (1368–1644) became increasingly commercialized during this era, and its ruling elite decided that porcelain was a product they could use to expand their market.

Europeans at this time were just beginning to encounter foreign commodities. Until the eighteenth century, the word "consumption" usually meant "loss" or "wasting away," but after the development of long-distance, international commerce, the word came to mean acquisition and ownership. With the rise of European consumerism in the sixteenth century, Chinese porcelain manufacturers discovered they could manipulate need to create demand.

As early as the Yuan dynasty (1279–1368), Islamic customers had imposed their decorative aesthetics on Chinese potters, who were willing to decorate their export wares with verses from the Koran and other images appealing to Muslim buyers. Chinese potters also adopted underglaze painting, an Islamic technique probably first used in the Middle East during the twelfth century, and they obtained the all-important cobalt-oxide pigment called "Mohammedan blue" from there as well. Thus, the blue and white porcelain that became synonymous with Chinese export porcelain was a multicultural product.

Traders in India had imported Chinese porcelain since at least the fifteenth century, and the Portuguese, who conquered Goa in the early sixteenth century, learned about porcelain there. The Portuguese goal was to control the spice trade to Asia then monopolized by the Islamic world. Portugal established direct contact with Beijing between 1517 and 1521, and their merchants successfully created the mechanics of the east–west trade in porcelain and other goods. The shipment of a small number of vessels decorated with the royal arms of King Manoel I of Portugal (1469–1521) marks the commencement of the blue-and-white porcelain trade between Asia and Europe.

The Dutch United Provinces, the sixteenth-century rival of the Portuguese Empire, also first discovered Chinese porcelain on the Indian continent in 1596. They had gone to Asia to wrest the lucrative spice trade away from their Iberian competitors. The first large shipment of Chinese blue and white porcelain to enter the Dutch United Provinces came from a captured Portuguese ship in 1602. The Dutch referred to the porcelain as *"kraakporselein,"* a word rooted in the type of Portuguese ship—the carrack—from which they were looted.

In response to the rising demand in Europe, the Ming ruler decided to transform the city of Jingdezhen in Jiangxi province from a market town into a major porcelain-producing, industrial center. Potters in Jingdezhen, who had made ceramics since early Ming days, had ready access to the two key ingredients needed to make thin-bodied, hard-paste porcelain: kaolin (fine, white) clay and feldspar.

The sixteenth-century thirst for Chinese porcelain had implications both in Europe and in China. Chinese potters were willing to use decorations that they did not understand but that they knew were desirable outside China. For their part, Europeans were so eager to obtain porcelain that they would accept pieces that Chinese consumers viewed as inferior. European consumers would even accept porcelain vessels with glaring flaws. A ewer made during the Zhengde period (1506–1521)—at the time of earliest Portuguese contact—attests to the European hunger to obtain porcelain. The vessel has the shape preferred by Muslims, but the decoration of the royal Portuguese coat of arms is painted upside down! Despite such obvious mistakes, elite European owners of porcelain used these scarce, exotic wares as symbolic markers of their wealth and high social standing.

For their part, the Spanish (and rival nations that captured Spanish ships) sent vast amounts of silver (mostly from Peru) to Asia, which the

Chinese eagerly sought. In exchange, Chinese potters—willing to peddle what they considered to be inferior goods—sold porcelain vessels by the hundreds of thousands to willing Europeans. Between 1602 and 1650, Europeans imported millions of vessels, with most of them going into the Dutch trade. Shipwreck excavations provide tangible proof of the huge number of porcelain objects exported from Asia.

Shortly after realizing that Chinese porcelain could stimulate demand, potters in Spain, Mexico, and Portugal decided to seek a share of the market by attempting to imitate Chinese porcelain with earthenware. Italian potters mass-produced earthenware vessels with Middle Eastern and North African designs in the fifteenth century, and European potters, particularly in the Dutch United Provinces, soon began their own attempts to duplicate Chinese export wares, but with little success.

European potters also painted their earthenware ceramics with designs they presumed were copies of Chinese motifs, but they often missed the mark by a wide margin. Since the potters had no direct experience with China or the Chinese, their decorations could be bizarre caricatures of Chinese motifs. European potters copied the concept of "the Oriental" rather than the detail of Asian artwork. One of the most popular decorations among the Dutch was the Wan-li pattern, characterized by a broad border painted with large blue chrysanthemums on an off-white background. These fake Chinese patterns were so popular that Dutch painters often including Wan-li vessels in their still-life studies (such as Hubert van Ravensteyn's *Still Life of a Flower, Glass, Stoneware Jug, and Walnuts in a Chinese Bowl on a Ledge*, painted around 1670).

One of the important features of ceramics as commodities, as demonstrated by the poorly made porcelain accepted by European consumers, is that objects could have entirely different meanings to purchasers than to producers and merchants. A porcelain vase could have a different value to each individual in the production–trade–use chain. The potter who made the vase may have understood it as having use value, meaning that it served the purpose of employment and created a livelihood. For the merchant, the vase had exchange value, meaning that it can be traded for something of equal or greater value. In a market economy, exchange value is often simply price, but in nonmarket societies, exchange value may be expressed as other objects (deer skins, shell beads, or horses). For the consumer, the porcelain vase may have had esteem or symbolic value, meaning that it can represent high social position, wealth, or access to scarce resources. Any single artifact—in this case, a sixteenth-century porcelain vase made in China—can assume many meanings.

The reason an artifact can assume different meanings to distinct individuals and social groups occurs because people who adopt new artifacts into their lives "contextualize" them. This means they impart their own meanings to them within their social, cultural, and historical setting. Understanding these diverse meanings requires a good deal of careful archaeological thinking. It demands that the archaeologist be thoroughly conversant with the culture, its history, and the nature of the culture's possible contacts with other cultures. Most archaeologists acknowledge consumption to be an active process, meaning that consumers do not simply purchase objects because they need them. People acquire all kinds of things sometimes simply because they want them. Desire (in this case, imparting esteem value to material objects) is an important element of modern consumption studies, and scholars of consumerism have examined how manufacturers and advertisers create desire.

Once an archaeologist has accepted desire as a possible motive for acquiring material objects, the key question is, What lies behind the desire, and how it is manifest in excavated artifacts from an abandoned settlement? These are always difficult questions to answer because of the diverse number of variables affecting motivation. The need to address them requires careful archaeo-thinking. An example from my experience is useful.

I spent several summers with students excavating nineteenth-century house sites in rural Ireland. Families who had been evicted during the Great Irish Famine (1846–1851) once lived in the houses we investigated. Many historians, using eyewitness accounts written both before and during those terrible years of hunger and disease, described how the Irish rural people, whom they termed "peasants," lived. A remarkable feature of just about every account, however, was a failure to mention the people's ceramics. This may seem like a trivial point, but archaeologists understand the significance of pottery and ceramics because they often contain important clues about a past historical culture. In terms of English ceramics specifically, a familiarity with them has implications for contacts with the outside world, changes in cultural perception, and the adoption or rejection of new customs.

Given that Ireland was next door to England—the nineteenth century's greatest producer of fine-bodied, white earthenwares—I wondered whether rural Irish families had ever been consumers of these ceramics. This was an important question because the image of the rural Irish as "peasants" carried with it the view that they were backward, traditional to a fault, and inward looking. Common wisdom held that they had used mostly handmade wooden bowls and woven baskets. The only exception was a large iron kettle, which they probably obtained in a local market. In this picture, Irish families had no use for imported ceramic plates, bowls, and teacups because they ate their meals from the iron kettle placed in the middle of the floor.

Based on my personal knowledge of the archaeology of enslavement in the New World, coupled with my having read accounts by other archaeologists about the material possessions of the enslaved, I refused to believe that Irish families would not have had at least some familiarity with imported English ceramics. The claim I wanted to investigate, therefore, was, "Irish families living in rural communities had some knowledge of and involvement with the English ceramics market." At the time, the archaeology of rural Ireland was just beginning, so no earlier studies were available to consult. Only excavation could provide the fresh information needed to assess the claim. The second site we studied, called Ballykilcline, in County Roscommon, provided important information.

At the height of its population in the 1840s, about 500 people lived at Ballykilcline. The community included 79 families, and the one on which we concentrated was the Nary family. They had lived in their two houses from about 1810 to 1848. They were evicted in 1848, sent to America, and settled in various locales throughout the country.

Our excavations revealed that the family had at least 100 different fine earthenware dishes in their two homes. (We excavated all of one house and a tiny portion of a second.) Over half of their dishes (51.4 percent) were imported from English factories (26.3 percent were Irish-made coarse utilitarian bowls and crocks, and 22.4 percent were unidentifiable). Included in the collection of imported wares were 21 different decorative techniques (including blue and green shell-edged plate fragments). Forty-three of the vessels were intended for table use (e.g., plate, small bowl, and tureen) and 44 for tea preparation and drinking (e.g., cup, saucer, and teapot).

This evidence made it clear that Irish farmers, at least at these two house sites, had access to and willingly accepted imported English ceramics. Subsequent excavations at six other house sites produced similar results. Clearly, Irish farm families were not isolated "peasants" stuck in tradition and refusing to accept the world of modern consumption.

The ceramics found at the Ballykilcline houses raised important questions about how rural Irish society had changed in the early nineteenth century. At the very least, it disputed the image of tradition-bound peasants. The ceramic evidence made it likely that at least some Irish farmers ate dinner from plates and drank tea (or other beverages) from teacups.

This evidence, even though of major significance from a cultural standpoint, did not answer the question, What had inspired the family's desire to own the imported wares? Up until the late 1960s or so, a common archaeological answer would probably have included acculturation. This would mean that Irish families had purchased English ceramics because they were becoming more English. Their ownership of English dishes provides tangible proof that they were accepting an English way of life and leaving their Irish ways behind.

As archaeological thinking has become more sophisticated, most archaeologists have abandoned the acculturation model as too simple. In the case of the Nary family at Ballykilcline, the idea of acculturation is especially difficult to accept because they, like all but two other families, were actively involved in a 16-year-long rent strike against the English Crown. Failure to pay rent, not the famine per se, was the reason the families were evicted. (Through a twist of fate, Queen Victoria was the community's landlady.) Rather than embracing England and Englishness, it seems the people were fighting against them. So why did they have English ceramics? Could it be so simple that the families were just looking to improve their living conditions by adopting the most modern dishes?

A possible clue to their motivation may come from research conducted by archaeologists working hundreds of miles away in the United States. At sites inhabited by African Americans and Native Americans during the eighteenth and nineteenth centuries, archaeologists have documented the active nature of consumption practices. Using material objects—even those that were mass-produced—individuals and groups can use material possessions to create images of themselves useful in the world around them. With equal economic resources, even discriminated-against ethnic and racialized groups can purchase the same kinds of objects as people in the socially dominant groups. This means that individuals and groups can use material things as active participants in their practice of social strategies.

Ceramics can play an important part in this process. As the availability of thin-bodied, white ceramics increased throughout the world (coming first from English factories but increasingly from American), ceramic dishes became a way for social groups and individuals to create, maintain, and even circumvent social boundaries. The use of ceramics to create meaning, boundaries, and identity moves the discussion to the concept of ceramics as ideas.

Ceramics as Ideas

We saw in the previous section that nineteenth-century ceramic manufacturers competed with one another to sell their goods as widely as possible.

Josiah Wedgwood (1730–1795) was an eighteenth-century master of doing just this, and he became fabulously wealthy as a ceramic entrepreneur.

Wedgwood, whom we first met in chapter 1, was one of the most successful ceramic producers in eighteenth-century Britain. He was so famous that wares from his factory were (and still are) highly prized objects. Hundreds of tourists visit his still-operating factories, and his name continues to inspire a sense of elegant style. The eighteenth-century public also valued his wares, and for many, his name was synonymous with English ceramics (even though he had many intensely competitive rivals). The value of owning his wares dramatically increased after Queen Charlotte commissioned a tea service in 1765 and a dinner service in 1766. Ever the shrewd businessman, Wedgwood called the pattern he made for her "Queen's Ware," knowing that the affluent English and colonial publics would purchase the ware in an effort to mimic the royal family.

One of the main characteristics of Queen's Ware was its whitish body. Beginning with Queen's Ware, the goal of British ceramics manufacturers was to produce wares as white as possible. They had this goal for two reasons. First, whiteness was a symbol of modernity, cleanliness, and the future. The idea of whiteness, expressed in mass-produced ceramics, became an idea of the times. Second, white-bodied ceramics, decorated with blue designs, could be made to resemble the much-sought-after Chinese export porcelain.

Up to the middle of the eighteenth century, most of the ceramics produced in Europe were thick-bodied wares. Three basic types existed: stoneware, coarse earthenware, and tin-glazed earthenware (called faience in France; delft in the British Isles and the Dutch United Provinces; majolica in Italy, Spain, and Mexico; and maiolica in Portugal). Stoneware, which is still widely made today, is a thick, heavy, gray-bodied ware, typically made into crocks, large jars, other types of storage vessels. Coarse earthenware, also still made today, is a thick-bodied ware often produced in the same vessel forms as stoneware, but potters also made other forms, such as milk pans and mixing bowls. Potters could leave these wares unglazed (like a terra-cotta flower pot) or glaze them, usually with earth-toned browns and greens and even black. Potters had been making coarse earthenware since at least the Middle Ages, so they were definitely not modern or forward-looking pieces. An eighteenth-century household with only these wares would look old-fashioned. Similarly, stoneware storage vessels would have no place in the dining area of a refined household. These wares belonged in the kitchen, the dairy, or the yard.

Potters in Europe began to make tin-glazed (lead glaze with tin oxide) earthenware vessels perhaps as early as the thirteenth century, but they were widely available by the beginning of the eighteenth century. In northern Europe, these wares had a thick, dull grayish-white surface. They were heavy and chipped easily, revealing their brick-red or buff-colored interiors.

Eighteenth-century consumers found another white, thin-bodied ware appealing—white salt-glazed stoneware (ca. 1715–ca. 1820)—but potters could never make it pale enough to match the whiteness of the highly desired Asian porcelains. The prime goal of European potters was to create a white-bodied ceramic that would look good when painted with blue decorations. Only in this way could they produce wares looking something like Asian porcelain but be much less expensive to purchase. A cheaper ware, if sold in high enough numbers, could still produce great wealth.

Wedgwood's formula for Queen's Ware did not spring from thin air. He worked feverishly for long periods to perfect it. He tried one mixture, discarded it as inferior, and then tried another formula until he obtained the desired result. His "Experiment Book" documents the many combinations of ingredients he used before deciding on the final formula. In his quest to make white ceramics, he even sent agents to America in search of clays that would fire like the fine-white porcelain clays from Asia. But in the end, Queen's Ware, though whiter than the earlier wares, was creamy rather than white.

Wedgwood called Queen's Ware "cream-coloured." (The archaeologists' and ceramic collectors' "creamware.") He had not yet produced a white-bodied ware to challenge Asian porcelain. In 1768, he wrote to his partner, stating, "With respect to the colour of my ware I endeavour to make it as pale as possible." Wedgwood was deeply concerned about the color of his product because he wanted a ware acceptable to consumers dedicated to modern ideas. He knew the whiteness of his cream-colored wares varied and understood that consumers wanted whiteness.

By 1790, the owners of at least eight competing factories were also attempting to produce a white ceramic. Potters used various names to distinguish their products from the others and to express the idea of whiteness, including "china glaze," "pearlware," and "pearl white." (Late eighteenth- and early nineteenth-century Europeans often associated pearls with Asia, and Hong Kong has often been referred to as "the pearl of the Orient.") The word "pearl," with its connotation of whiteness, became a generic term for white-bodied ceramics during the era. The new wares—pearlwares—were much whiter than the cream-colored wares, and they had the advantage of being able to accept blue decorations and thus mimic Asian porcelain much better than the creamier wares.

By the early nineteenth century, a number of English potters had begun to experiment with producing even whiter bodies, using new formulas and firing their vessels at high temperatures. By this time, the English ceramics industry, localized in Staffordshire, dramatically expanded. In 1710–1715, the Staffordshire potteries had about 500 employees working in 47 different "potworks." In 1769, about 300 potteries operated with about 6,000 workers, and by 1835 the number of employees had grown to about 20,000. The potteries of Staffordshire occupied six separate towns. Old photographs reveal thick clouds of smoke billowing from the forest of bottle ovens (ceramic kilns named for their shape) blotting out the sun (figure 7.4). What we today call industrial pollution people in the past perceived as progress. Author George Orwell, visiting the Staffordshire "pottery towns" in 1936, observed, "Right in among the rows of tiny blackened houses, part of the street, as it were, are the 'pot banks'—conical brick chimneys like gigantic burgundy bottles buried in the soil and belching their smoke almost in your face."

This brief overview of the English ceramics industry reveals that English potters were increasingly dedicated to producing the whitest wares possible. The appeal of cream-colored ware, though a major innovation when first introduced, had lost consumer confidence as other potters introduced whiter wares. Consumers believing in the promise of modernity wanted white-bodied dishes on their dinner tables and in their drawing rooms.

The subject of porcelain—and the whiteness they inspired—is not complete without mentioning its Chinese companion: tea. In colonial American history, no commodity was imbued with more symbolism than

Figure 7.4.   Nineteenth-century image of bottle kilns at work in Staffordshire, England. From a postcard printed by Shaws of Wolstanton.

tea. We take it for granted today, but just remembering the Boston Tea Party, even if knowing little about it, suggests that tea had a special place in Anglo-American history.

English and American consumers became acquainted with Chinese tea early in the seventeenth century, but its use was controversial. One commentator said that tea would make "the bold and brave become dastardly, the strong become weak, the women become barren," but another described it as "the preserver of beauty." As the controversy over tea's effects waned (or was simply ignored), tea became the English national drink. English teatime is today famous throughout the world.

Historical evidence indicates that the practice of drinking tea spread rapidly through all levels of European society. In eighteenth-century England, the wealthy drinkers of tea invented a tea-related etiquette that required owning and knowing the "proper" use of material culture, including ceramics. Thus, tea—in a formalized setting—became a social beverage, one that carried with it ideas of politeness, order, and hospitality. Having a successful tea party meant presenting the right objects in the perfect setting. (Remember the chaos of the poorly organized tea party in *Alice in Wonderland*?)

The ideal eighteenth-century English (and colonial American) tea set included, in matching porcelain, at least a dozen cups and saucers, a container for milk or cream, a teapot, a pot for hot water, a bowl for used tea leaves, and a sugar bowl. (Sugar, a related commodity and status symbol, has its own story.) Also needed were a set of silver tongs, spoons, and butter knives. The perfect tea also required a fine wooden tea table (preferably mahogany) and linen tablecloths and napkins. So important was the proper presentation of tea that many wealthy individuals had their portraits painted seated around a formal tea setting.

Our excavations at Ballykilcline revealed the presence of a minimum of 44 separate tea-related ceramic vessels. The teacups and teapots in the Nary houses provide strong evidence that they were at least acquainted with the beverage, even though the conduct of the upper-class tea ceremony is less likely to have occurred. With the available evidence, then, from the site of my excavations, we can propose two alternative interpretations:

1. the Nary family obtained English ceramics (including tea wares) because they wanted to feel more English and possibly to project this image to their neighbors, or
2. the Nary family obtained English ceramics for some reason having nothing to do with Englishness.

The nature of archaeological research means that no one will ever be able to determine the Narys' motivation with 100 percent certainty. Given their role in the rent strike against the English Crown, the plausibility seems remote that they sought to project an image of Englishness. Other historical evidence supports the implausibility of this interpretation. The Narys, like their neighbors, professed Roman Catholicism rather than English Anglicanism, and they were Celtic by heritage rather than Anglo-Saxon. Religion and heritage were two important factors in the history of English (and later British)–Irish relations. Many individuals with Protestant, Anglo-Saxon backgrounds denigrated the Irish people for their "heathen" beliefs and their non-English bloodlines. These contributing factors must be taken into account when providing an interpretation of the Narys' interest in English ceramics.

The central point is that archaeologists interpret artifacts, in this case fine earthenware ceramics and porcelain, in different ways. With time, further excavations will help archaeologists sharpen their understanding of pre-famine life in the Irish countryside. Changes in interpretations are bound to occur. This is a normal part of thinking to some purpose in archaeology.

Archaeologists strive to produce interpretations about the past having the highest degree of plausibility using the evidence at hand. Different individuals and social groups in the past may have owned identical sets of dishes (and other pieces of material culture), but each group may have interpreted the objects differently based on a host of possible circumstances and situations. Personal possessions can be used to symbolize all manner of things, extending from the simple ability to own something valuable to feelings of identity. The task of the careful archaeological thinker is to sift through all the available evidence and devise a reasonable interpretation, fully understanding that future research is likely to modify or even to destroy the original interpretation.

Continue Reading

Archeology and Consumption

Mullins, Paul R. 1999. *Race and Affluence: An Archaeology of African America and Consumer Culture.* New York: Springer.

———. 2011. *The Archaeology of Consumer Culture.* Gainesville: University Press of Florida.

Orser, Charles E., Jr. 1996. Beneath the Material Surface of Things: Commodities, Artifacts, and Slave Plantations. In *Contemporary Archaeology in Theory*, edited by Robert Preucel and Ian Hodder, 189–201. Oxford: Basil Blackwell.

Pezzarossi, Guido. 2014. Camouflaging Consumption and Colonial Mimicry: The Materiality of an Eighteenth and Nineteenth-Century Nipmuc Household. *International Journal of Historical Archaeology* 18: 146–74.

Ballykilcline

Duffy, Peter. 2007. *The Killing of Major Denis Mahon: A Mystery of Old Ireland*. New York: Harper.

Dunn, M. L. 2008. *Ballykilcline Rising: From Famine Ireland to Immigrant America*. Amherst: University of Massachusetts Press.

Orser, Charles, E., Jr., ed. 2006. *Unearthing Hidden Ireland: Historical Archaeology in County Roscommon*. Bray: Wordwell Press.

Scally, R. J. 1995. *The End of Hidden Ireland: Rebellion, Famine and Emigration*. New York: Oxford University Press.

Chinese Export Porcelain

Carswell, John, Edward A. Maser, and Jean McClure Mudge. 1985. *Blue and White: Chinese Porcelain and Its Impact on the Western World*. Chicago: University of Chicago Press.

Dillon, Michael. 1992. Transport and Marketing in the Development of the Jingdezhen Porcelain Industry during the Ming and Qing Dynasties. *Journal of the Economic and Society History of the Orient* 35: 278–90.

Gordon, Elinor, ed. 1979. *Chinese Export Porcelain: An Historical Survey*. New York: Main Street/Universe.

Le Corbeiller, Clare, and Alice Cooney Frelinghuysen. 2003. Chinese Export Porcelain. *The Metropolitan Museum of Art Bulletin* 60, no. 3: 1–60.

Wei Ji. 2006. *The Art of Chinese Ceramics*. Translated by Sylvia Yu, Julian Chen, and Christopher Malone. San Francisco: Long River Press.

Consumption

Appadurai, Arjun. 1996. *Modernity at Large: Cultural Dimensions of Globalization*. Minneapolis: University of Minnesota Press.

Bourdieu, Pierre. 1984. *Distinction: A Social Critique of the Judgement of Taste*. Translated by Richard Nice. Cambridge, MA: Harvard University Press.

Inda, Jonathan Xavier, and Renato Rosaldo, eds. 2007. *The Anthropology of Globalization: A Reader*. 2nd ed. Malden, MA: Blackwell.

McCracken, Grant. 1990. *Culture and Consumption: New Approaches to the Symbolic Character of Consumer Goods and Activities*. Bloomington: Indiana University Press.

Miller, Daniel. 2012. *Consumption and Its Consequences*. London: Polity.

Slater, Dan. 1997. *Consumer Culture and Modernity*. Cambridge: Polity.

English and American Tea Drinking

Fromer, Julie E. 2008. "Deeply Indebted to the Tea-Plant": Representations of English National Identity in Victorian Histories of Tea. *Victorian Literature and Culture* 36: 531–47.

McCants, Anne E. 2008. Poor Consumers as Global Consumers: The Diffusion of Tea and Coffee Drinking in the Eighteenth Century. *Economic History Review* 61, suppl. S1:172–200.

Moxham, Roy. 2004. *Tea: Addiction, Exploitation, and Empire*. London: Robinson.

Roth, Rodris. 1961. *Tea Drinking in 18th-Century America: Its Etiquette and Equipage*. Washington, DC: United States National Museum, Smithsonian Institution.

English Ceramics

Godden, Geoffrey A. 1964. *Encyclopedia of British Pottery and Porcelain Marks.* New York: Crown.

Hunter, Robert R., Jr., and George L. Miller. 1994. English Shell-Edged Earthenware. *The Magazine Antiques* 145: 432–43.

Kowalsky, Arnold A., and Dorothy E. Kowalsky. 1999. *Encyclopedia of Marks on American, English, and European Earthenware, Ironstone, and Stoneware (1780–1980).* Atglen, PA: Schiffer.

Majewski, Teresita, and Michael J. O'Brien. 1987. The Use and Misuse of Nineteenth-Century English and American Ceramics in Archaeological Analysis. In *Advances in Archaeological Method and Theory,* vol. 11, edited by Michael B. Schiffer, 97–209. Tucson: University of Arizona Press.

Reilly, Robin. 1989. *Wedgwood.* 2 vols. New York: Stockton.

Thomas, John. 1971. *The Rise of the Staffordshire Potteries.* New York: Augustus M. Kelley.

General

Bahn, Paul. 1989. *Bluff Your Way in Archaeology.* Partridge Green: Ravette.

Hayes, Katherine Howlett. 2013. *Slavery before Race: Europeans, Africans, and Indians at Long Island's Sylvester Manor Plantation, 1651–1884.* New York: New York University Press.

Rathje, William, and Cullen Murphy. 1992. *Rubbish! The Archaeology of Garbage.* New York: HarperCollins.

Schiffer, Michael Brian, with Andrea R. Miller. 1999. *The Material Life of Human Beings: Artifacts, Behavior, and Communication.* London: Routledge.

Thinking to Some Purpose
Archaeological Research and Critical Thinking

8

HROUGHOUT THIS BOOK, I have made frequent reference to Professor Stebbing and her little book *Thinking to Some Purpose*. At first, you may have been surprised by the age of this book. After all, it appeared at the start of World War II, and that was a long time ago. But if we consider that the concept of critical thinking goes back to the ancient Greek philosophers, we can see that 1939 was not all that long ago after all. An important point to remember is that the principles and concepts the professor presented in her little book are still relevant today. The usefulness of her ideas extend from everyday life to all fields of scholarly endeavor, including archaeology. They are especially important in archaeology because the archaeologist's interpretations rely on educated suppositions, well-grounded assumptions, and informed inferences.

The concept of critical thinking may be an old one, but it remains a prominent issue today, as scholars, educators, and politicians debate it. A Google Scholar search returns over 3.2 million publications about the subject! The number will undoubtedly continue to grow as increasing numbers of people express concern about the state of education in the United States. Critical thinking skills of the sort promoted by Professor Stebbing have gained special prominence because, for one thing, many publicly funded schools have begun to direct their teaching toward success in assessment tests rather than toward the intellectual skills needed to confront and solve life's many problems. In a 2011 article in the *New York Times*, Ellen Galinsky, author of *Mind in the Making: The Seven Essential Life Skills Every Child Needs*, said, "It's not just knowing the information.

. . . It's knowing how to find the answers to the questions that is the basis of critical thinking."

Galinsky directed her comment to the importance of critical thinking skills in general, but she just as easily could have been speaking about archaeology. Archaeology is a difficult field simply because human social and cultural life was (and is) complex. If you imagine the great diversity in the activities, practices, and customs carried out by people around the world today—from Mongolian herders to American factory workers—you can begin to understand the breadth of the puzzle that archaeologists face. If you consider all the cultures that have lived on Earth since the beginning of human life, you can see why unraveling the history of humanity gets increasingly murky. The archaeologist's inability to be an eyewitness to the past—to see past life actually happening—demands careful, logical thinking.

We can quickly appreciate the wisdom of Galinsky's point by returning to where we began: with the Great Pyramid. Clearly, having information about the size, shape, and interior design of the pyramid is not enough. Pseudo-archaeologists and professional archaeologists have the same basic information but devise opposite interpretations from it. What good is knowing everything possible about the physical nature of the Great Pyramid—its size, the number of its chambers, the time it took to build, and its relation to other structures—if we could not think critically about its meaning? And, when thinking about its meaning, we must consider the pyramid's context both in ancient Egypt and in the world today. How has the perception of the structure changed over time, and why?

Only by thinking critically about all the known elements of the Great Pyramid can analysts move beyond mere speculation and toward valid interpretations. Knowing the information without thinking is simply not good enough; archaeologists also must know how to answer some of the most interesting questions with the available empirical evidence. Speculations lack plausibility, and interpretations must be grounded in the possible.

The scholarship surrounding critical thinking is vast. Myriad topics can be explored, and we have touched on only a few here. The ones presented in this book are especially pertinent to good archaeo-thinking. One additional, extremely important issue, however, remains to be presented. This concerns the danger of bad archaeo-thinking.

Does faulty thinking do any harm? What is the harm of arguing that the Great Pyramid was used as a nuclear facility? Why not just consider it a fanciful and fun claim and let it go at that? Why must archaeologists always attempt to spoil the public's fun by arguing against the role of space aliens in human history? Aren't there two sides to every story, and who says that professional archaeologists must be right?

The Danger of Faulty Archaeo-Thinking

Faulty reasoning may be harmful. In *The Miniature Guide to Critical Thinking: Concepts and Tools*, Richard Paul and Linda Elder provide a useful guide to the dangers of poor reasoning. Stating why they believe critical thinking to be so important, Paul and Elder acknowledge that it is human nature to think, but thinking, if done illogically, may be biased and hurtful.

Shoddy thinking has profound implications for archaeology because distortions of history can cause significant harm. Many of the wildest hypotheses—such as the nuclear pyramid idea—are fairly harmless. They do violence to Egyptian history to be sure, but information about ancient Egypt is so readily available that anyone can easily discover how professional scholars understand the history of Egypt's many ancient dynasties. Even the most basic knowledge about ancient Egyptian culture should quickly allow anyone to disregard the nuclear hypothesis as totally unrealistic.

Unfortunately, interpretations presented by individuals not thinking clearly extend far beyond the world of fringe archaeology. If only pseudo-archaeologists engaged in promoting fantastic interpretations, the history of the world would not change. Their views would continue to frustrate and annoy professional archaeologists, but anyone with a sincere interest in history and archaeology would quickly understand the many fallacies in their interpretations. Unfortunately, people in power have occasionally been able to pervert the course of history because of their biased and even bizarre views of the human past.

Examples from pseudo-archaeology appear throughout this book because the practitioners' flaws are so easy to spot, being based strictly on speculation. But more serious interpretations employing shoddy thinking also exist. These more developed interpretations have distorted, misrepresented, and ignored important pieces of history.

The most dangerous and poorly thought-out interpretations in archaeology have been used to silence, erase, or misrepresent the past. Some examples rely on fringe ideas, and these can be dismissed without much effort. More dangerous, however, has been the advancement of harmful ideas in professional archaeology—ideas and interpretations that were accepted or at least tolerated for a period of time. Ideas, concepts, and interpretations change as new information is made available, but the effects of damaging distortions may last for many years.

Two examples will suffice to illustrate the danger of bad archaeological thinking. The first comes from a site called Great Zimbabwe, while the second involves the archaeological efforts of professional Nazi archaeologists. In both cases, powerful people used biased thinking to distort history. These are extreme examples, but their prominence aptly demonstrates the ill effects that may occur when archaeo-thinking is abused.

Silencing the African Past

In the annals of archaeology, no better example exists to demonstrate the dangers of faulty thinking than Great Zimbabwe. Located in the Republic of Zimbabwe in southern Africa, Great Zimbabwe is sub-Saharan Africa's largest and arguably its most dramatic ancient site. Zimbabwe means either "houses of stone" or "venerated houses." Both names are accurate.

The site lies among gently rolling hills and is composed of a series of oval-shaped, dry-laid stone walls between 4 and 17 feet (1.2 and 5.2 meters) thick and about 34 feet (10.4 meters) tall at their highest. The site covers almost 198 acres (80.1 hectares) and incorporates a complex of stone walls encircling stone houses, raised platforms, and stairways. A few nonstone buildings, made from a mixture of clay and fine gravel, appear among the stone structures. Rounded bastions sit along walls here and there, and some sections have stone slabs arranged in decorative chevron patterns. Narrow alleyways meander between high stone walls. The most spectacular building is the Conical Tower (figure 8.1). This solidly built turret is 18 feet (5.5 meters) around and extends 30 feet (9.1 meters) in the air. Great Zimbabwe is a marvel of architectural engineering, and in 1986 the United Nations recognized it as a World Heritage Site.

The site is located in Mashonaland, a region occupied by Cecil Rhodes's powerful British South Africa Company in September 1890. Rhodes, a mining magnate of vast wealth and power, was a committed believer in the righteousness of the British Empire and was prepared to do whatever he could to advance its goals and aspirations in southern African. First and foremost, the colonization of Mashonaland was meant to extract the region's mineral wealth for the benefit of his company. The cultural heritage of the region was not Rhodes's concern unless it suited his larger aims. Being the most powerful person in the region, he was able to bend its history and archaeology to his goals. He began with Great Zimbabwe.

About 20 years before Rhodes had arrived in the region, a German geologist had located the massive archaeological site. He was as amazed as anyone who has seen it ever since. The geologist, knowing nothing about the history of the region and its people, decided after some reflection that

Figure 8.1.   Late nineteenth-century image of the Conical Tower at Great Zimbabwe. Photo by Mrs. J. T. Bent, 1891. Courtesy National Archives of Zimbabwe.

the site must be somehow related to the Phoenicians, the Queen of Sheba, and King Solomon. He believed that black-skinned Africans could have had nothing to do with it even though they may have visited it after its builders had abandoned it. From the very beginning of the Europeans' knowledge of the site, they equated it with nonlocal people. They made the same logical error as the early scholars who equated the earthen mounds of the eastern United States with the Lost Tribes of Israel, the Phoenicians, and others from outside North America (see chapter 1). In both cases, the interpreters assumed that indigenous people, whom they viewed as racially inferior to white Europeans, could not build complex structures. Even if they had the know-how, these biased thinkers figured that native leaders would never be powerful enough to encourage or coerce large numbers of people to spend time building massive structures.

Biased observers visiting Great Zimbabwe soon compared the site's Elliptical Building with a seventh-century BCE temple associated with the Queen of Sheba in faraway Yemen. Others observed that the chevron pattern on the walls was similar to a pattern on a temple depicted on a Roman coin. Such similarities must be a reflection, they thought, of cultural association. Thus, they made the error of equating similar-looking things to the same producers rather than imagining that individuals in two cultures can have the same ideas without being in contact with one another.

By the time Rhodes appeared in the region, archaeologists had generally decided the Phoenicians had nothing to do with the site, but they held on to the idea that it must be connected to biblical history. In fact, in 1905, R. N. Hall—who spent two and a half years exploring the site—proposed that the Conical Tower was "the truest evidence of Baal worship." Baal was an ancient pagan god mentioned in the Bible. The biblical association of the majestic ancient site fit Rhodes's colonialist plans perfectly because it removed the site from local African history and placed it squarely within Judeo-Christian tradition. The speculative history created a veneer of fantasy that reinforced the Europeans' colonial designs for the entire continent.

When professional archaeologists began to excavate Great Zimbabwe in the mid-twentieth century, it was clear to them that the builders and inhabitants of the buildings were a succession of indigenous peoples. These cultures needed no help from the Phoenicians, the Queen of Sheba, or even wise King Solomon. Excavations revealed a sequence of five periods of occupation extending from about the eleventh to the fifteenth centuries CE, with some deposits being both earlier and later in date. Archaeologists used standard methods of analysis to provide detailed chronologies of the pottery, architecture, and soil layers at the site. Their research provided concrete evidence that the history of the peoples who built, inhabited, and finally left the site composed a rich cultural mosaic.

The so-called "exotic interpretation" of Great Zimbabwe (that non–sub-Saharan Africans built it) is an example of biased thinking. It privileges the aspirations and hopes of a foreign power over those of a local people. It silences what might be learned about past actuality and creates false chronicles. Its biased thinking is fueled by speculation and wishful thinking. If the early scholars had been interested in doing so, they could have explored the true history of Great Zimbabwe despite the fact that Rhodes held total control over the country that would bear his name. The nonlocal interpretation, however, suited his colonist needs, and scholars—seeking access to the site and funds to study it—would have found it difficult (and perhaps even impossible) to challenge the interpretation he preferred. In fact, R. N. Hall said that the Government of Rhodesia had given him the "privilege to explore the Great Zimbabwe." Access to the site was a privilege granted by Rhodes himself.

The exotic hypothesis, which erroneously came to be called the "Zimbabwe controversy," rests on two biased assumptions:

1. That Africa had no history of its own that did not include Europeans
2. That sub-Saharan Africans could never have built the magnificent site

Misguided scholars have advanced this kind of biased thinking for many years whenever spectacular archaeological sites have been discovered. The "Mound Builder controversy" presented in chapter 1 is an exact duplicate of the "Zimbabwe controversy." In neither case did a real controversy exist: the exotic, nonlocal peoples whom early archaeologists identified as the possible builders—Israelites, Phoenicians, Egyptians, and Tatars—never had anything to do with the structures in question. Just like with Great Zimbabwe, the only mysteries revolve around how the people built the structures, how long they lived there, and what had happened to them. These questions require dedicated research and serious archaeo-thinking, not speculation and guesswork.

Unsurprisingly, a site like Great Zimbabwe—with its unique architecture and long history—has challenged the interpretive talents of many professional archaeologists. Once they had righted the history of the site once and for all, the people of Zimbabwe adopted it as a national symbol. The Conical Tower appears in the country's national coat of arms. The use of this ancient archaeological site as a visible symbol of national pride demonstrates how thinking to some purpose in archaeology can impact the contemporary world. Archaeological interpretations are not for archaeologists alone.

Nazi Archaeology

You might be surprised to learn that some of what you've seen in the Indiana Jones movies has a kernel of truth. Stripped of the fantastic elements needed for cinematic effect, the movies do reveal little snippets of actual dangerous archaeo-thinking. The Nazis really did send expeditions of archaeologists and physical anthropologists in search of the Holy Grail and to Tibet to discover the Aryan birthplace. The archaeology conducted by Nazi archaeologists was exaggerated and faked in one of the most egregious examples of archaeological fraud ever perpetrated. German National Socialists—Nazis—had a program of archaeological research that consciously set out to present false histories, chronicles that would demonstrate their greatness at the expense of others. Their era is a dark stain on the history of archaeological research.

Heinrich Himmler, the head of the powerful SS (*Schutzstaffel*, or protection squadrons) and an occultist who believed he was the reincarnation of Saxon King Heinrich I (who ruled 919–936 CE), was the architect of the Nazi archaeological program. In 1935, he created the *SS-Ahnenerbe* (Ancestral Heritage). One of the organization's main tasks was to study German history, which of course included archaeology. Hitler had little use for archaeology as a research subject, but, understanding its value as propaganda, he allowed it. Himmler was a true believer in the theory of German racial superiority, and the archaeologists of *Ahnenerbe* were expected to provide concrete evidence substantiating his racialist interpretation of German greatness. Much of this required modifying or even falsifying excavated evidence.

One of the goals of the Nazi regime was to replace Germany's Christian practices with an invented pagan religion based on myth and imagination. *Ahnenerbe* archaeologists were charged with discovering runic symbols on ancient pottery and other objects to legitimize the long history of this symbolism and its association with the German people. The swastika and the SS lightning bolts are the most well known symbols the Nazis adopted.

The Nazis' research into symbolism, though totally misguided, represents a tame use of archaeology. The use of runes and other seemingly ancient symbols supported the Nazis' cause of creating invented tradition, but such practices were not dangerous in and of themselves, though they certainly represented something sinister. Much more serious was the Nazis' perversion of archaeological research to support their theory of Germanic racial superiority.

The archaeologists who worked for *Ahnenerbe* often conducted respectable, systematic excavations. The problem was not always with their field methods but with their interpretations. As archaeologists working for the fascist regime, they were expected to provide evidence to support Nazi ideology. Providing backup for interpretations resting on faulty, politically preordained thinking required the archaeologists to mold their interpretations to the ideology rather than letting the evidence guide their interpretations. They knew their interpretation before going into the field to excavate a site. Nazi archaeologists might conduct a well-run, systematic excavation but interpret the findings in concert with the mandated racial theory.

One Nazi archaeologist, while excavating a settlement inhabited by a culture he termed "the battle-axe people," found weapons he decided were used for offensive warfare. Having made this interpretation, he then concluded that the love of weapons was a Germanic trait stretching back several thousand years into the past. Not finding shields in association with the axes, he next decided that ancient Germans had no interest in protective weapons. This had to mean that their fierce attitude to war had been conditioned by their blood. On discovering chain mail and helmets, however, he concluded that these were emblems of rank rather than pieces of defensive armor! Seen from today's vantage point, we can see that his interpretations were perfectly in agreement with Germany's offensive wars against its neighbors. The archaeologist simply adapted his archaeological interpretation to suit contemporary politics. He knew before he had even begun the study that he would mold his conclusions to fit Nazi ideology.

In 1941, Himmler saw pictures of what archaeologists then called the "Venus figurines." These statues are ancient carvings in wood and bone depicting women with exaggerated breasts, hips, and buttocks (figure 8.2). Archaeologists are still puzzled by them and do not know whether they are self-portraits, religious objects, pieces of art, or some combination. They do know that they date to the Upper Paleolithic era (about 30,000 years ago). Today's archaeologists might be puzzled by the meaning of the figurines, but Himmler most certainly was not. Thinking them to be accurate representations of primitive ancient peoples, he concluded that they provided support for his Germanic thesis. Because archaeologists found these figurines beneath more recent "Germanic" deposits, Himmler decided that the objects had been produced by primitive peoples who had been destroyed thousands of years ago by more powerful, racially superior German invaders. He believed that the exaggerated features of the women provided tangible proof of racial inferiority.

Using this pseudohistory for support, Himmler argued that it was only right that the twentieth-century Germans should conquer all the "lesser

Figure 8.2.   The Upper Paleolithic "Venus" of Willendorf in the Natural History Museum, Vienna, Austria. Photo by Don Hitchcock, donsmaps.com. Used by permission.

peoples" who surrounded Germany. He believed that archaeology helped demonstrate that racially superior peoples have always ruled over the less "racially fortunate."

The ideas presented by the Nazis, many of which used archaeology for support, were based on extremely dangerous, biased thinking. Rather than move from evidence to interpretation, the Nazis began with their interpretation (that the Germans were racially superior to everyone else) and made the evidence conform to it. They were ideologically unwilling to let the evidence modify or replace their preordained interpretation. Archaeologists who sought to present ideologically free interpretations were dismissed from their positions and not allowed to practice archaeology.

The pseudohistory of the Nazi regime was the official history of the German people from 1933 to 1945. The Germanic theory of racial superiority was a "truth" that dare not be denied during those terrible years. Archaeology, manipulated and cheapened, was merely one tool they could use to make their awful case. To combat this history and set the record straight, a number of archaeologists have recently begun to excavate Nazi prison camps. This research will counter the propaganda and lies perpetrated by the *Ahnenerbe*.

Final Thoughts

The site of Great Zimbabwe and the practices of the Nazi archaeologists demonstrate the dangers that can lurk within poorly designed or fraudulent interpretations of the past. Regrettably, many more examples exist. What I have tried to show in this book is that archaeological research is complicated because human cultures are complicated. There are no easy shortcuts to understanding human history; archaeological research requires knowledge, dedication, fairness, and clear thinking. The bogus interpretations of pseudo-archaeologists and politically motivated scholars do harm because they distort history. Invented histories obscure the fascinating realities of the human past by drawing instead on the fantastic and the improbable. Some "histories," such as the atomic pyramid interpretation we began with in chapter 1, are so ridiculous that they are easily dismissed. They exist simply as silly interpretations that only the most gullible take seriously. They are merely amusing fantasies. Other invented histories, such as those concerning Great Zimbabwe, offer dangerous distortions. These more serious distortions, by denying the realities of the African past or by promoting racial superiority, retard the advancement of archaeological knowledge. By not thinking to some purpose, the promoters of such interpretations seek to send archaeological research back into the speculative era of the nineteenth century.

Good archaeo-thinking has the power to promote knowledge in significant ways. But archaeo-thinking is neither easy nor necessarily straightforward. It takes dedication and an eagerness to learn the real history of human life on planet Earth. I hope this little book has given you the skills to become a master archaeo-thinker.

Continue Reading

Critical Thinking

Galinsky, Ellen. 2010. *Mind in the Making: The Seven Essential Life Skills Every Child Needs*. New York: HarperCollins.

Parker-Pope, Tara. 2011. School Curriculum Falls Short on Bigger Issues. *New York Times*, September 6, D5.

Paul, Richard, and Linda Elder. 2006. *The Miniature Guide to Critical Thinking: Concepts and Tools*. Tomales, CA: Foundation for Critical Thinking. http://www.criticalthinking.org/files/Concepts_Tools.pdf

Great Zimbabwe

Fontein, Joost. 2006. *The Silence of Great Zimbabwe: Contested Landscapes and the Power of Heritage*. London: UCL Press.
Garlake, P. S. 1973. *Great Zimbabwe*. London: Thames and Hudson.
Hall, R. N. 1905. The Great Zimbabwe. *Journal of the Royal African Society* 4: 295–300.

Nazi Archaeology

Arnold, Bettina. 2006. "Arierdämmerung": Race and Archaeology in Nazi Germany. *World Archaeology* 38: 8–31.
Arnold, Bettina, and Henning Hassmann. 1995. Archaeology in Nazi Germany: The Legacy of the Faustian Bargain. In *Nationalism, Politics, and the Practice of Archaeology*, edited by Philip L. Kohl and Clare Fawcett, 70–81. Cambridge: Cambridge University Press.
McCann, W. J. 1990. "Volk und Germanentum": The Presentation of the Past in Nazi Germany. In *The Politics of the Past*, edited by Peter Gathercole and David Lowenthal, 74–88. London: Unwin Hyman.

Index

Note: Page numbers in italics refer to tables, photographs, and other illustrations.

historians and history: archaeology and, 28–30, 82, 113–15; biased thinking in, 155–56, 158–63; culture and, 82, 106; false, 160–63; interpretations about, 18, 23–24; of language, 122–23; meanings of, 111–13; science's relationship to, 7–8, 22, 113–14; seventeenth-century, 107–8; use of term, 58. *See also* antiquarians; facts, historical

historical archaeologists and archaeology, 47, 82, 104; artifact studies by, 93–94; inferences made in, 69, 86, 87; use of term, 113–14

Hitler, Adolf, 160

Homer, 14

Howell, Martha, 116

humanities, 7–8, 30, 114. *See also* social sciences

hypotheses. *See* claims

Iceland, Irish monks' voyages to, 127, 130

ideas: artifacts as, 136; ceramics as, 145–50

identity, 145, 150

India, involvement in porcelain industry, 141

Indiana Jones movies, 133, 160

indigenous peoples, 18, 23, 112, 113, 125–26, 158. *See also* African Americans and Africans; Celtic peoples; Native Americans

induction, 76–84; arguments by, 70, 83–84, 87, 90; from authority, 78–83, 116; by enumeration, 76–78

inferences, in historical archaeology, 69, 86, 87

interpretations: in archaeo-thinking, 5–7, 30–44; of artifacts, 18, 49, 133–36, 150; competing, 10, 11, 44, 154; consensus view, 82–83; contrasted with detection, 8;

diverse, 45–47, 51; ethnographic, 92; evidence-based, 5–10, 13, 20, 24, 130–31, 150; exotic, 159; fact selection for, 53, 66–67; historical and cultural, 18, 23–24; Nazi ideology, 160–63; plausibility of, 44–45, 49, 60, 134, 150, 154; speculative, 13, 79–80, 154. *See also* fantasy, interpretations based on

Ireland: early travels to North America from, 79, 95–96, 124–31; excavations in, 143–45, 149–50

Italy, pottery from, 142, 146

Jefferson, Thomas: and authorship of Declaration of Independence, 120, 122, 123; excavations in Virginia, 13–14

Jewish people, Native-American connection to, 14, 15

Jordan, Michael, 79, 81

Kahneman, Daniel, 5

Kidd, Kenneth and Martha, classification of colonial trade beads, 62–66, *64*

King Philip's War (1675–1678), 107

King William's War (1689–1697), 107

Knossos (Crete), excavations at, 91, *92*

knowledge: through excavations, 41–42; growth of, 83, 134, 135, 163

Kroeber, Alfred, 58–59

language, historical context of, 122–23

L'Anse aux Meadows (Newfoundland), Norse settlement at, 124

Leone, Mark, 65, 66

Lhwyd, Edward, 93, 107–8

light, speed of, 35, 36

logic, archaeo-thinking and, 22, 69–88, 134; abductive, 86–87; analogy and, 91; deductive, 70–73,

About the Author

Charles E. Orser, Jr., research professor at Vanderbilt University, is an anthropological historical archaeologist who investigates the modern world as it was created after about 1492. He gained experience in historical archaeology in the United States (eastern and southern), Europe (Ireland), and South America (Brazil). He is the author of over 90 professional articles and a number of books, including *Historical Archaeology*, *A Historical Archaeology of the Modern World*, *The Archaeology of Race and Racialization in Historic America*, *Race and Practice in Archaeological Interpretation*, *Unearthing Hidden Ireland: Historical Archaeology at Ballykilcline, County Roscommon*, and *A Primer on Modern-World Archaeology*. He is the founder and editor of the *International Journal of Historical Archaeology*. His research interests include post-Columbian historical archaeology; practice, network, and socio-spatial theory; globalization and consumerism; social inequality; discrimination; and poverty. His regional interest is the Atlantic world.